LEAPS

for

BEGINNERS

How to Use Long-Term Options to Build Wealth, Protect Your Portfolio
and
Make Big Gains
with Limited Risk

FREEMAN PUBLICATIONS

TABLE OF CONTENTS

INTRODUCTION:

ONE OF MY GREATEST TRADES

April 4th started like any other morning. I was feeding my 9-month-old daughter her breakfast, scrolling through my phone to catch up on the overnight market news. Yes, you can judge my parenting skills, but sometimes you have to multitask.

What I saw made me nearly drop the spoon. The world was reeling from Trump's Liberation Day tariff announcements. The SPY was down 4.9%, after a 3.9% decline the night before. The Nasdaq was down over 10%. And global markets were suffering too. But as I dug deeper into the carnage, something caught my attention.

Semiconductors had dropped 15% overnight, despite being completely exempt from the proposed tariffs. The market was throwing the baby out with the bathwater, punishing what I consider the most important industry in the world simply because investors were panicking.

This wasn't rational. This was opportunity.

Within an hour, I'd made my decision. The semiconductor sector would recover from this overreaction - I was certain of that. The question wasn't if, but when. It could take weeks, months, or even over a year for the market to come to its senses.

That's exactly why I chose SOXL, a leveraged semiconductor ETF, and more importantly, why I bought an 18-month LEAPS call instead of the stock itself. I had no idea when the rebound would happen, but I was confident it would occur within 18 months. The LEAPS gave me time for my thesis to play out without the pressure of short-term expiration dates.

Figure 1: Chart of SMH alongside SOXL trade entry (source: Stockanalysis.com)

This was a small, calculated bet - exactly the kind of risk-controlled position that LEAPS are designed for.

The Power of Patience and Leverage

What happened next validates everything I believe about LEAPS investing. Within a week Trump had announced a 90 day pause on tariffs. Within 30 days the SPY was back to where it was on April 2, and by May 13th, it turned positive for the year. The semiconductor sector began its rally back to new highs.

Just 66 days after that panicked morning feeding my daughter, I closed my SOXL position for a **413% gain.** It was my best trade in two years, and it happened because I had the right tool for the job.

Here's what made this trade work - I had stock-like upside potential with only a fraction of the capital at risk. Instead of buying $10,000 worth of SOXL stock, I controlled the same amount of upside for just $3,400. Plus when the position moved in my favor, the leverage amplified my gains.

8

This wasn't luck - it was thesis… plus time… multiplied by the right tool. And I'm not the only one who understands how powerful the right tool can be. Hedge funds, pension funds, and university endowments use LEAPS for exactly the same reasons I do: capital efficiency, flexibility, and defined risk.

When you buy a LEAPS call, you know exactly how much you can lose (the premium you paid) while maintaining unlimited upside potential. You get leverage without margin calls, time without the pressure of weekly expirations, and the ability to participate in major moves without tying up massive amounts of capital.

So if you get nothing else from this book - just remember this. **When used correctly, LEAPS can provide greater returns with *less* risk than a traditional stock investment.**

This book will show you how to apply these same principles in your own portfolio. You'll discover how to identify the right opportunities, select the optimal LEAPS contracts, and manage positions for maximum profit while controlling risk.

Whether you're looking to enhance returns on your existing portfolio, generate income through advanced LEAPS strategies, or simply want another tool for building long-term wealth, this book will give you everything you need to succeed.

The semiconductor trade was just one example. By the time you finish reading, you'll have a complete system for using LEAPS to potentially transform your investment results - all while maintaining the kind of lifestyle that lets you focus on what really matters, like feeding your kids breakfast without worrying about the markets.

Let's get started.

Oliver El-Gorr
Founder and CEO, Freeman Publications
London, September 2025

IF YOU HAVE NO EXPERIENCE WITH OPTIONS

The remainder of this book assumes that you understand the basics of how options work. So you know what a strike price is, understand expiration dates and other fundamentals of the option markets.

---

3 factors which affect option prices

- Difference between strike price and market price
  - Strike price = agreed price
  - Market price = current price of the asset

- Time until expiration
  - Prices generally don't fluctuate much until 30-45 days before expiration, this is known as time decay

- The volatility of the asset
  - The more volatile the asset, the higher option prices will be... because there is a wider range of scenarios which could occur

CAPITAL GAINS MULTIPLIER

If you don't, that's totally fine as I've made an in-depth tutorial called Options 101 which you can find in the bonus resources section of this book at freemanpublications.com/bonus - it's 100% free

Chapter 1

LEAPS DEMYSTIFIED

In 2008, when the global financial system was unraveling, hedge funds and pension funds weren't just selling assets, many were quietly using LEAPS to control risk. University endowments, sovereign wealth funds, even Fortune 500 treasuries have relied on them for decades to gain stock exposure with a fraction of the capital.

These aren't lottery tickets, in fact they are one of the most trusted tools in institutional finance.

What Are LEAPS?

LEAPS stands for **Long-term Equity Anticipation Securities**. Despite the intimidating name, they're simply call or put options with expiration dates of one year or longer.

They work in the exact same way as a regular option, with calls giving you the right, but not the obligation to take ownership of a stock at a fixed price, within a given time period.

But a single detail, the gift of time, is what makes them different. While most options expire in 30-60 days, LEAPS give you 12-36 months for your investment thesis to play out. That one factor changes everything.

You can use LEAPS to be bullish (with calls) or bearish (with puts). You can buy them for capital upside or sell them for income. You can use them to protect existing positions or to gain leveraged exposure to stocks you believe will rise over time.

With a deep in-the-money LEAPS call option, you can mimic stock ownership almost 1:1 but with only a fraction of the cash outlay. This is why institutional investors love them, because they free up capital for other investments while maintaining stock-like exposure.

Side note: In video content you may hear me refer to a single trade as "A LEAP Option" rather than "A LEAPS Option". This is simply because it's easier to say (especially when you have to say it 30 or 40 times in an hour.) The correct written version, which will be used throughout this book will refer to a single trade and multiple trades as LEAPS.

Three Key Advantages Over Owning Stock

Capital Efficiency

Imagine you want exposure to Google (GOOG). At $210 per share, 100 shares would cost $21,000. Instead, you could buy a deep in-the-money LEAPS call with a $160 strike price, expiring 15 months out, for about $6,490–$6,545. (Depending on liquidity, you can often buy closer to the mid-point, the "Mark" price, rather than paying the full ask price. On heavily traded names like Google this is almost always possible, saving you $50–$60 per contract.)

Figure 2: GOOG option chain for LEAPS calls (source: Tastytrade)

◇ The LEAPS option behaves like owning 80 shares. An 0.80 delta LEAPS is like owning 80 shares out of 100, you don't get the full $1 move, but you've also put much less at risk.

◇ You control nearly the same upside for one-third the initial cost.

◇ The other $14,455 stays free to earn 4% in T-bills, to diversify, or to hold as dry powder.

Professionals call this capital efficiency.

Why 80 Delta = 80 Shares

Each LEAPS contract represents 100 shares of stock, but delta tells you how closely your option actually tracks those shares in practice.

A call with 1.00 delta moves dollar-for-dollar with 100 shares - if the stock rises $1, your option gains $100 in value. But a call with 0.80 delta moves about 80 cents for every dollar the stock moves, which means it behaves more like owning 80 shares than 100.

Here's how this works in real terms: if you buy a deep in-the-money LEAPS with 0.80 delta and the stock moves up $1, your LEAPS gains approximately $80 in value. If the stock drops $1, your LEAPS loses about $80. You're getting 80% of the stock's movement, not 100%.

The higher the delta, the more stock-like your option becomes. Deep in-the-money LEAPS typically trade between 0.80-0.90 delta, which is why we say they behave like owning 80-90 shares rather than a full 100 shares.

Delta itself changes over time due to gamma effects, but as a practical rule of thumb for position sizing and risk management: your delta multiplied by 100 gives you the approximate stock-equivalent exposure you're carrying.

This is why we target high-delta LEAPS for stock replacement strategies - you want that stock-like behavior, not the lottery ticket characteristics of low-delta options.

Defined Risk

If you buy the stock, your theoretical max loss is 100% (company goes to zero). With LEAPS, your maximum loss is limited to the premium you paid. If you paid $6,700 for your Google LEAPS, that's your worst-case scenario, no margin calls and no forced liquidation.

Leverage Without Margin

Traditional leverage means borrowing from your broker and risking margin calls. With LEAPS, leverage is baked in. You get amplified upside, but your downside remains capped at the premium. In other words: you get leverage *without* sleepless nights.

Myth Busting: Why LEAPS Aren't Gambling

When I first started writing about LEAPS, some readers accused me of hypocrisy. After all, I've spent years warning people about the dangers of short-term options and the "Robinhood casino."

The truth? Buying short-term options (<30 days) and buying LEAPS (12–36 months) are completely different animals:

◇ Buying Short-Term Options (Gambling)

◇ Massive time decay as value melts away daily.

◇ Require perfect timing (because the market may take too long to recognize your thesis is correct, so your option can expire worthless before the stock finally moves your way).

◇ 95% of retail traders lose.

◇ Buying LEAPS (Investing)

◇ Minimal time decay in year 1.

◇ Behave like stock ownership (0.80–0.90 delta ≈ 80–90 shares).

◇ Give your thesis multiple quarters, even years, to play out.

◇ Used by pensions, hedge funds, and endowments.

This isn't roulette. This is investing with a smarter tool.

In theory, it sounds symmetrical. In practice, it isn't:

◇ **Stocks rise more often than they fall.** Over long periods, markets grind upward. That means you're fighting against the natural trend when you buy long-dated puts.

◇ **Upside is limited.** A stock can only go to zero, so your maximum gain is capped. With calls, upside is theoretically unlimited.

> Many new traders look at puts and think, *"If I can bet on a stock going up, why not just bet on it going down?"*

◇ **Timing is harder.** Down moves tend to be sharper and shorter. If your put expires before the crash, you can still lose 100% of the premium even if you were "right" eventually.

◇ **Psychological drag.** Holding a long-dated bearish bet for months while the stock chops sideways or rises slightly is emotionally draining. Most beginners cut the trade too early or abandon their system.

So while LEAPS puts *do* have a place, like for portfolio insurance, which we'll cover later in the book, they're not where beginners should start. For most new investors, it's far easier to learn the mechanics of LEAPS with bullish call positions first, then add puts later once you're comfortable managing risk.

Using Leverage the Right Way

Leverage gets a bad reputation (cue Charlie Munger's "liquor, ladies, and leverage" quip). But with LEAPS, you're using leverage *intelligently*.

Let's walk through an example with Amazon:

◇ Stock price: $230.

◇ 100 shares = $23,000.

Or...

◇ Buy a LEAPS call, $165 strike, 20 months out, delta ~0.80 = $8,680.

◇ That one contract behaves like ~80 shares.

Now let's compare returns:

◇ If AMZN rises 15% → stockholders make 15%. LEAPS holder makes ~22%.

◇ If AMZN rises 40% → stockholders make 40%. LEAPS holder makes ~91%.

Why does this happen? Because with LEAPS, you're only putting a fraction of the stock's full cost on the table. In this example, you controlled ~$23,000 worth of Amazon with just $8,680. That smaller initial outlay means your *percentage gains (or losses)* are magnified relative to owning the stock. This is the essence of leverage, you're getting almost the same dollar move as stock ownership, but measured against a much smaller investment.

◇ Stockholders gain $3,450 on a 15% move → 15% return on $23,000.

◇ LEAPS holders gain ~$1,900 on the same move → ~22% return on $8,680.

And remember: if AMZN tanks, your max loss is $8,680. You'll never get a margin call or lose more than you put in.

Scenario	Stockholders (100 shares @ $230 = $23,000)	LEAPS Holders (1 contract @ $165 strike, premium $8,680)
AMZN +15% ($265)	+$3,450 → +15% return	+$1,900 → +22% return
AMZN +40% ($322)	+$9,200 → +40% return	+$7,900 → +91% return
AMZN -100% ($0)	-$23,000 → -100% loss	-$8,680 → -100% loss (capped at premium paid)

Anticipating Your Objections

"Aren't options risky?"

Options are tools. Used incorrectly, yes, they're risky. With LEAPS, risk is capped upfront.

"Don't I have to watch my positions every day?"

No. You'll check your positions once a month at most. LEAPS are designed for busy people.

"Isn't this gambling?"

Gambling is betting on an earnings report with a weekly call option that expires in three days. LEAPS give you 18-24 months for your investment thesis to play out, so they are more like stock ownership with extra efficiency.

"What if I'm wrong about timing?"

That's exactly why LEAPS work better than short-term options. You can be wrong about timing and still profit if you're right about direction. Companies don't move in straight lines, but LEAPS give you time for the overall trend to emerge.

The Mindset Shift

If you've been thinking about options as short-term trading tickets, it's time to completely reframe your approach. LEAPS aren't about catching quick moves or timing the market perfectly - they're about something much more systematic and sustainable.

The process starts with identifying businesses you genuinely want to own for the long term, companies with strong fundamentals and competitive advantages that you believe will compound value over years, not months. Then you use LEAPS to gain stock-like exposure to these businesses with significantly less capital, freeing up money for diversification or other opportunities while maintaining similar upside potential. More importantly, you define your risk in advance through careful position sizing and stop-loss planning, so you know exactly what you can lose before entering any trade.

The key psychological shift is embracing patience as a strategic advantage rather than a burden. Markets rarely move in straight lines and even the best companies experience temporary setbacks, earnings disappointments, or periods of consolidation that can last quarters.

With LEAPS, you have the luxury of being wrong in the short term while still being right about the long-term direction, allowing your investment thesis to play out over multiple business cycles rather than fighting against the natural volatility of markets.

Why This Chapter Matters

My SOXL trade from the introduction worked not because of luck, but because I had 3 things in place

1 - The right thesis (semiconductors were oversold)

2 - Enough time (18 months) for markets to normalize.

3 - The right tool (a LEAPS call that amplified my gains while capping my risk)

That's the formula: **thesis + time + tool.**

In the next chapter, I'll show you how professionals plan trades systematically, because even with the right tool, you need a plan that keeps you from making rookie mistakes.

Key Takeaways

◇ LEAPS = Long-term Equity Anticipation Securities (options with 12–36 month expiry).

◇ Work like regular calls/puts but with more time.

◇ 3 advantages vs stock: Capital efficiency, defined risk, leverage without margin.

◇ Myth-busting: LEAPS ≠ gambling (minimal decay early, stock-like behavior).

◇ Key mindset shift: LEAPS are about systematic investing, not short-term speculation.

Chapter 2

PLANNING A TRADE LIKE A PRO

I've long thought I was a diligent trader, because unlike my living room, my trading plans have always been very organizing and systematic. But then I met Anthony-James Owen, and I realized there were levels to this game. Anthony, who won our Trader of the Year award in 2024, is one of those rare gems who is both A) A smart smart, and very successful trader in his own right and B) knows how to distill his ideas to a point where a laymen can understand them.

I'll resist the urge to make a German efficiency joke, partly because he's only half-German, but I will say that Anthony showed me how a true trading pro operates. He's a former hedge fund manager Anthony, who managed money through the dot-com crash and the 2008 financial crisis. He's overseen high-net-worth portfolios and family office accounts worth hundreds of millions. In his world, no trade ever happened without a very extensive written plan.

When assisting me in teaching students, Anthony would (very politely) grill them

"Where's your entry criteria? Your stop-loss? Your take-profit target? Your position sizing? What exactly will you do if the stock gaps down another 10% tomorrow morning?"

"You trading <u>plan</u> is far more important than your trade *idea*" - he would say

His insights changed everything about how I approach using LEAPS.

Why Retail Traders Blow Up With LEAPS

As I mentioned, while working at his fund, Anthony would regularly oversee trades where one bad day would swing the P/L by millions of dollars. In his world, no trade ever happened without a written plan.

Yet here many investors (including me in my early days) stand, ready to risk thousands of dollars on a "feeling" about Netflix or put 50% of their portfolio into a Tesla short because they think Elon Musk has lost it.

The harsh reality is that most retail traders approach LEAPS the same way. They jump into trades based on…

Gut feelings about where a stock is headed…

Hot tips from financial media or social media…

FOMO when they see a stock making big moves…

Revenge trading after a previous loss…

What they don't have is what every professional has: a systematic approach to trade planning that removes emotion from the equation.

The 5-Step Institutional Playbook

After many humbling conversations with Anthony, I started studying how institutions actually plan their trades. What I discovered was a surprisingly simple framework that any individual investor can use.

Every professional trade plan contains five core elements:

Idea Origin: Why are you looking at this trade? What's your thesis?

Market Context: What are the broader market conditions telling you?

Entry Criteria: What must be true before you get in?

Exit Criteria: What tells you to take profits or cut losses?

Position Sizing: How much of your portfolio are you risking?

Let me walk you through each element using real examples.

Step 1: Idea Origin

Your trade idea has to come from somewhere concrete, not just a hunch. The best LEAPS trades typically fall into three categories:

Fundamental catalysts: Earnings growth acceleration, margin expansion, new product launches, or management changes that could drive long-term value creation.

Technical setups: Chart patterns showing potential breakouts, trend reversals, or stocks holding key support levels during market weakness.

Macro themes: Sector rotations, policy changes, interest rate shifts, or economic cycles that could benefit specific industries or companies.

Once again, I can't stress this enough, "some guy online told me it was a sure thing" is not a good enough reason to put your hard earned cash into a stock (LEAPS or no LEAPS)

Step 2: Market Context Check

Before entering any LEAPS trade, you need to understand the broader market environment. You'll have a much easier time making money by being bullish in a bullish market than a bearish one.

This doesn't require complex analysis - just a few key indicators

VIX Level: Below 15 suggests calm markets favorable for bullish trades. 15-20 is slightly elevated but not a major concern. Anything above 25 is a sign you should wait (because of inevitable IV decline, which we'll talk about later)

Market Trend: Is the S&P 500 above or below its 200-day moving average? Bullish LEAPS work better in bull markets (the trend is your friend, after all)

Sector Strength: How is your target sector performing relative to the broader market? You want to be buying strength, not trying to catch falling knives.

Step 3: Technical Confirmation

Even if you're not a technical analysis expert, a few simple checks can dramatically improve your LEAPS timing:

Trend Filter: For bullish trades, make sure the stock is trading above its 50-day moving average. This simple rule eliminates many losing trades.

Support Levels: Identify key support levels from recent lows. These become your stop-loss reference points.

Resistance Levels: Mark significant resistance levels that could serve as profit-taking zones.

Figure 3: *Support and Resistance levels for Amazon (AMZN) - with the stock trading at $228, there is resistance at $240 with support level at $215 and $211. As the $211 support level is also the 200 day moving average, this would be a good support level to place your stop loss for the trade (source: tradingview.com)*

Step 4: OptionStrat - Your New Secret Weapon

Here's where most traders wing it, but professionals use tools to model their trades before risking real money.

One of my personal favourites is OptionStrat.com. This is a free platform that lets you visualize exactly how your LEAPS (and other options trades) will perform under different scenarios.

Here's my exact process...

1. Go to OptionStrat.com and select "Build > Long Call"
2. Input your ticker and choose an expiration 12-24 months out
3. Select a deep ITM strike with a delta between 0.80-0.90
4. Switch to "Table View" to see contract values at different stock prices
5. Adjust the stock price slider to your identified support level
6. Note the option price at that stock price - this becomes your stop-loss
7. Calculate your total dollar risk: (Entry Price - Stop-Loss Price) × 100

This process takes five minutes and gives you precise risk parameters before you trade.

Quick clarification for beginners: support is simply a price zone where the stock has repeatedly bounced before. Think of it as the "floorboards" beneath the price. So if the stock smashes through that floor, something fundamental may have changed in your thesis. For example, if support is at $50, I'll usually place my stop slightly below (say $48–$49) to avoid being shaken out by short-term noise.

> Note: We have a video tutorial for using Optionstrat (along with many others) available as a free bonus for this book. Just head on over to freemanpublications.com/bonus

Step 5: Entry and Exit Rules

Entry Criteria:

⬦ For an ideal balance of capital efficiency and probability of profit you want a delta minimum of 0.70, preferably 0.80-0.90

⬦ For a maximum delta level, don't pay more than 50% of the stock price for your LEAPS option. So if it costs $20,000 to buy 100 shares of the stock, your LEAPS call should be no more than $10,000

⬦ Days to expiration (DTE) minimum of 12 months, ideally 18-24 months

⬦ Avoid entering right before earnings unless your thesis is earnings-driven

Exit Rules:

⬦ Profit target: A simple rule would be a +100% gain from entry option price

⬦ Stop-loss: As calculated from OptionStrat at support break

⬦ Time exit: Roll or close 60 days before expiration to avoid rapid time decay

A note on exit strategies

Successful LEAPS trading isn't just about picking the right stock, it's about knowing **exactly when to exit**. Here's a framework you can apply to every trade...

Take-Profit (TP):

⬦ **Fixed Rule:** Close the trade when the option price has doubled (**+100% gain**).

⬦ **Trailing Rule:** Once you're up **+50–100%**, raise your stop so you keep at least half your gains.

◇ **Thesis Rule:** Exit when your catalyst has fully played out (e.g., slowing revenue, multiple expanion complete).

Stop-Loss (SL):

◇ **Support Rule:** Identify a clear stock support level. If it breaks, your thesis is wrong, and you should exit.

◇ **Option Price Rule:** Use OptionStrat to find what your LEAPS is worth at that support level. That becomes your stop-loss number.

◇ **Time Rule:** Roll or exit 60 days before expiration if your thesis hasn't played out.

The key: TP locks in your upside. SL protects your downside. Both should be written into your plan *before* you enter any trade.

Step 6: Position Sizing

This is where most traders get themselves into trouble. The rule is simple: never risk more than 2-5% of your total portfolio on any single LEAPS trade. So if you have a $100,000 portfolio, you shouldn't be risking more than $5,000 on each LEAPS trade.

Portfolio Size ($)	Max $ at Risk using 5% rule
50,000	2,500
100,000	5,000
250,000	12,500
400,000	20,000
500,000	25,000
600,000	30,000
750,000	37,500
1,000,000	50,000

1,500,000	75,000
2,000,000	100,000
3,000,000	150,000

If your calculated dollar risk is $1,200 per contract and you want to risk a maximum of $3,600, you buy three contracts. No exceptions.

Case Study: The Robinhood Trade That Made 38% in 11 Days

Let me show you how this framework worked on a recent trade. In early 2024, Anthony noticed unusual momentum in Robinhood (HOOD) after a positive news article about their crypto business expansion.

Idea Origin: Fundamental catalyst - expanding crypto offerings during a potential crypto bull market

Market Context: VIX at 18, S&P 500 above 200-day MA, fintech sector showing relative strength

Technical Setup: HOOD breaking above 50-day MA on high volume, clear support at $12

OptionStrat Analysis: 18-month LEAPS call, 70 strike, 0.80 delta, stop-loss at $1,800 per contract if stock hit $12

Position Size: $4,000 total risk (two contracts)

Outcome: +38% gain in under two weeks when the momentum continued

The trade worked because he had a plan. More importantly, he would have known exactly what to do if it hadn't worked.

You might be wondering - why take profits at 38% when the usual target is 100%?

In this case, the stock ran quickly in a short time. By banking early, Anthony freed up capital to redeploy elsewhere rather than letting it sit tied up for another year. That decision gave him a much higher "annualized return" on that capital.

Avoiding Emotional Landmines

Having a written plan eliminates the emotional decisions that destroy most traders.

Revenge trading after a loss becomes impossible when you have systematic entry criteria.

Moving stops lower to avoid taking a loss violates your pre-written rules.

Exiting early on the first sign of profit goes against your predetermined targets.

The plan keeps you disciplined when emotions try to take over.

Your Trading Plan Template

Before you make another LEAPS trade, write down:

1. Why am I making this trade? (Idea origin)
2. What are current market conditions? (VIX, trend, sector strength)
3. Where will I enter? (Price level, delta, DTE)
4. Where will I exit for a profit? (Target percentage)
5. Where will I exit for a loss? (Stop-loss level)
6. How much am I risking? (Dollar amount and portfolio percentage)

If you can't answer all six questions, you're not ready to trade.

Remember, the best LEAPS strategy in the world is worthless if you put it on the wrong company at the wrong time with the wrong risk management.

And if you want a downloadable trading plan – then you can grab that in the resources section at freemanpublications.com/bonus

In the next chapter, we'll dive into exactly how to identify the companies worthy of a LEAPS position, starting with the fundamental analysis that separates winning trades from expensive lessons.

Key Takeaways

◇ Most retail traders blow up because they skip planning.

◇ **5-Step Institutional Playbook**:

◇ Idea Origin (fundamental, technical, or macro catalyst).

◇ Market Context (VIX, market trend, sector strength).

◇ Technical Confirmation (support, resistance, moving averages).

◇ Trade Modeling (OptionStrat to define risk & stop-loss).

◇ Entry/Exit Rules (profit targets, stop-losses, time exits).

◇ Position sizing: Never risk >5% of portfolio on one LEAPS trade.

Chapter 3

WHY FUNDAMENTALS MATTER FOR LEAPS

L ate 2020 was peak pandemic-induced market mania. C3.ai was one of the many companies that had just gone public, at a huge valuation multiple. The headlines were abuzz that this company would revolutionize how enterprises used AI. I mean, they even had the perfect ticker symbol.

Retail forums, YouTube videos and Twitter were buzzing with predictions of $300 price targets. The stock jumped from around $42 at IPO to $183 in just a few weeks.

I was watching the chart climb and thinking what every trader thinks during these moments: "If this keeps going, it's life-changing money."

The momentum was intoxicating. It felt like every day brought new highs, new analyst upgrades, new reasons why artificial intelligence would transform everything. C3.ai was positioned as the first pure-play AI stock that would ride the wave to incredible heights. Remember, this was pre-Chat GPT, so even the AI hype was still in its early days.

But when I dug into the actual numbers behind the hype, the story fell apart quickly. Revenue growth was *slowing*, not accelerating. The company was burning cash at an alarming rate. Competition was intensifying from tech giants with deeper pockets. The fundamentals didn't match the story Wall Street was selling.

I passed on the trade. Six months later, C3.ai had crashed back near its IPO price. Anyone who bought LEAPS at the peak learned an expensive lesson: over 12-24 months, fundamentals always win.

The Time Horizon Changes Everything

This is why fundamentals matter so much for LEAPS investing. With short-term options, you might get lucky riding momentum or catching a quick bounce. But LEAPS give you 12-24 months for your investment thesis to play out, and over that timeframe, the underlying business performance determines your success.

One key element you can always fall back on is this. There are only 2 ways a stock price can increase in the medium and long term

Expansion of a key business metric (sales/earnings) - either through raw performance like earnings per share (EPS) increases or revenue growth, or through share buybacks when a company uses their cash to purchase their own shares on the open market, decreasing the number of shares available and increasing EPS.

Expansion of the multiple of said business metric (P/S or P/E ratio) - the premium that shareholders are willing to pay for each dollar of sales or earnings.

That's it. Every stock that doubles, triples, or goes up 10x does so through some combination of these two factors. Understanding this changes how you evaluate LEAPS candidates completely.

It's also important to note that without the first element (fundamental improvements), the second (valuation spike) won't last.

Knowing this, it gives us 2 categories of business that make ideal candidates for LEAPS.

Existing great businesses that will continue to be great

These are the companies that already have everything working in their favor - strong moats, growing markets, excellent management, and consistent execution. Think Microsoft, Meta, or ASML. They're not broken and don't need fixing. They just need time to compound their advantages.

The challenge with great businesses is that everyone knows they're great, so you rarely get them at bargain prices. But LEAPS allow you to participate in their continued success with less capital than buying the stock outright. When Microsoft trades at 25x earnings instead of its usual 30x, that might be your opportunity to get leveraged exposure to one of the world's best businesses.

These companies typically deliver steady, predictable growth. You're not looking for dramatic turnarounds or explosive moves - just the reliable compounding that comes from owning excellent businesses. Your LEAPS thesis is simple: this great company will continue being great, and the market will eventually pay full price for that greatness.

Turnarounds

These are stocks that have been beaten down, but you believe will recover. Maybe they've lost market share, faced temporary headwinds, or made strategic mistakes that are now being corrected. The key word here is "temporary" - you need evidence that the problems are fixable *and* that management is fixing them.

Turnaround situations offer more upside potential because you're buying when sentiment is poor and expectations are low. But they also carry more risk because your thesis might be wrong - sometimes companies are beaten down for good reasons that won't be resolved.

The best turnaround LEAPS candidates already show early signs of improvement: margins stabilizing, market share losses slowing, new products gaining traction, or cost-cutting programs showing results. You want to see at least 1-2 quarters of confirming data before committing capital.

Deckers Outdoor is a perfect turnaround example. The company had become too dependent on UGG boots, but they are successfully diversifying with HOKA running shoes and improving their operational efficiency. The fundamentals were inflecting positive, but the stock price hadn't yet recovered from the early 2025 downswing.

Figure 4: *DECK turnaround recommendation (Source: Kit)*

Note: The full analysis of Deckers Outdoor (DECK) is available in the bonus section at <u>freemanpublications.com/bonus</u>

Both categories can work well with LEAPS, but they require different approaches to timing, position sizing, and risk management. Great businesses give you more margin for error but less upside potential. Turnarounds offer bigger gains but demand more careful analysis and tighter risk controls.

But your question at this point is, how on Earth do you *consistently find* these stocks?

Needles in a Haystack

There are infinite ways to find stocks, but only 3 reliable ones.

Insider information - which is illegal and will land you in federal prison

Your own circle of competence and knowledge of an industry - the Warren Buffett approach of investing in what you understand

Stock screeners - using software to systematically filter thousands of companies based on specific metrics

Since we're not interested in orange jumpsuits, and most of us don't have deep expertise in multiple industries, stock screeners become our primary tool for finding LEAPS candidates.

Screener Setups That Surface Hidden Gems

My personal favorite screener is stockanalysis.com. It's fast, has no ads, and it's free (although you can't save the screener on the free version). More importantly, it focuses on the fundamental metrics that actually matter for LEAPS investing, rather than getting bogged down in dozens of technical indicators that don't predict long-term performance.

The Circle of Competence Advantage

Before we dive into screeners, let's acknowledge the power of investing in what you know. If you work in healthcare, you might spot trends in medical devices before they show up in earnings reports. If you're in technology, you understand which software companies have real competitive advantages versus those riding hype cycles.

Peter Lynch made this famous with his "invest in what you know" philosophy. He found some of his best investments by observing consumer trends - noticing that Dunkin' Donuts always had long lines, or that his wife kept buying more Hanes pantyhose.

The key is translating your industry knowledge into investable insights. Just because you work at a company doesn't automatically make it a good LEAPS candidate. You still need to run it through the fundamental analysis we covered in the previous chapter.

Now using stockanalysis.com - we can set up screeners for each type of LEAP candidate

Screener 1: Great fundamentals

High level criteria

- ◇ Is this company more efficient at turning assets and investments into returns than its rivals?
  - ◇ Metrics like ROE, ROA and ROIC can signal a strong moat
  - ◇ I also use share change <3% so we only have companies that are shareholder friendly (not companies like Gamestop that dilute their shares every other month)

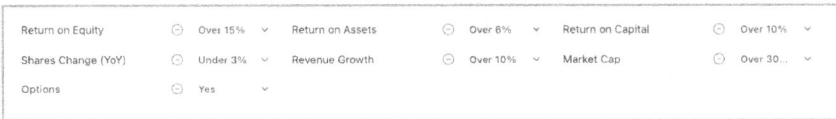

Return on Equity		Over 15% ∨	Return on Assets		Over 6% ∨	Return on Capital		Over 10% ∨
Shares Change (YoY)		Under 3% ∨	Revenue Growth		Over 10% ∨	Market Cap		Over 30... ∨
Options		Yes ∨						

Figure 5: Fundamental Screener (source: stockanalysis.com)

This screener brings up the names you'd expect like Nvidia, Meta, Amazon and Netflix.

But it also brings up some smaller quality names like Rollins Inc. (ROL), the nation's leading pest control company and Sprout's Farmers Market (SFM), which has quietly become one of the leading retail stocks over the past 5 years. Both of which would be high on my LEAPS candidate list.

Screener 2: Potential turnarounds

High level criteria

- ◇ Are these company's worst days behind them?
  - ◇ Metrics like debt/equity and current ratio ensure a solid cash position (we don't want debt laden stocks)
  - ◇ Buyback yield signals the company's willingness to buyback shares (another shareholder friendly metric)

Market Cap	⊖	Over 10B	⌄	Debt / Equity	⊖	Under 0.5	⌄	Current Ratio	⊖	Over 1	⌄
Net Cash (Debt)	⊖	Over 0	⌄	Buyback Yield / Dilution	⊖	Over 0%	⌄	EPS Growth Next Year	⊖	Over 5%	⌄
Options	⊖	Yes	⌄								

Figure 6: Turnaround screener (source: stockanalysis.com)

It's important to note that not every stock on this screener is a turnaround play, names like Nvidia, Taiwan Semiconductor and Applied Materials are obviously not turnaround stocks. This is why it's important to go to the performance tab and sort by price change (either YTD or 1Y depending on when you are running the screener)

Then you will get your list of potential turnaround candidates. The screenshot below shows the top 5 most beaten down names as of August 11, 2025.

Symbol	Company Name	Market Cap	Stock Price	% Change	Change YTD	Change 1Y ⌃
REGN	Regeneron Pharmaceuticals, Inc.	57.71B	556.56	1.94%	-21.87%	-50.80%
DECK	Deckers Outdoor Corporation	15.39B	103.74	3.25%	-48.92%	-30.08%
GFS	GlobalFoundries Inc.	18.23B	32.84	3.86%	-23.47%	-24.83%
ACN	Accenture plc	148.91B	237.87	-0.31%	-32.38%	-24.68%
LEN	Lennar Corporation	32.24B	124.47	3.27%	-5.71%	-24.26%

Figure 6: Snapshot of candidates from turnaround screener (source: stockanalysis.com)

Now before you rush off and place those entry orders, it's important to validate these ideas, so in the next chapter I'll show you how to do just that.

Over 12–24 months, **fundamentals drive outcomes**, not hype.

Key Takeaways

◇ Stock prices rise via 1 of 2 categories

◇ Growth in EPS/revenue (or buybacks).

◇ Expansion of valuation multiple (P/E, P/S).

◇ Two types of stocks which work best for LEAPS: **Great businesses** and **Turnarounds**.

◇ Stock screeners help identify candidates (ROE, ROA, ROIC, debt/ equity, buybacks).

◇ Fundamentals always win over time.

Chapter 4

YOUR VERY OWN RESEARCH ASSISTANT

Once you've identified potential LEAPS candidates through screening, the real work begins. Numbers on a spreadsheet can tell you what happened, but they can't tell you *why* it happened or whether it's likely to continue.

This is where qualitative research becomes critical. You need to understand the business model, competitive dynamics, management quality, and industry trends that will determine whether your 12-24 month thesis actually plays out.

The problem is that traditional fundamental analysis can take hours per company - reading through 10-K filings, earnings transcripts, analyst reports, and industry research. Most individual investors don't have that kind of time, which is why, inside our Capital Gains Multiplier program, we spend 2 full modules on this alone, as well as weekly calls sharpening our swords.

But the good news is, if you're short on time, this where AI comes in. Used correctly, artificial intelligence can compress hours of research into minutes, giving you institutional-quality analysis without the institutional-level time commitment.

So today I'm going to give you the 80/20 of research using AI tools. Using these tools you will be able to get a good understanding of the company's longer term potential.

First Principle of Using AI: Garbage In, Garbage Out

Most people don't know how to use AI tools because most people don't know how to prompt the tool (meaning, how to ask questions). Because with AI, your results will only be as good as the quality of your prompts.

So going to ChatGPT and asking "should I buy LEAPS on [STOCK]" is not a good idea.

Without additional prompting, AI models lack context and nuance, so if you don't provide any, then you will always get a high-level, reasonably "good sounding" answer, but with little relevance to your situation.

The good news is that these AI models can be trained to give you good answers, if you provide the right inputs.

Before we go further, if you don't understand what a company does - DO NOT BUY LEAPS ON IT.

These are longer term trades with multiple earnings calls and news events. If you don't understand the company then you won't know how to interpret news, you won't understand quarterly earnings, and your decisions will solely be influenced by stock price and daily chatter on news websites and social media.

I cannot stress this enough - if you don't understand the company, don't buy it.

Fortunately, we can use AI to help. Here's a prompt you can use.

"Explain [Company name] to me like I am a 16 year old on my first day of business class"

We did this on a live student call for LRCX, and the difference between this prompt, and the base answer was night and day.

Base answer

Lam Research Corporation (NASDAQ: LRCX) is a leading supplier of equipment and services used to manufacture semiconductor wafers. Its tools and systems are critical in the "front end" of chip production —the steps that build and shape the transistors and interconnects on silicon—while also addressing back-end processes like wafer-level packaging and advanced packaging technologies. Key product areas include:

- **Thin film deposition**: Systems that lay down conducting (e.g. copper) or insulating (dielectric) layers with atomic-scale precision, using techniques such as chemical vapor deposition (CVD), electrochemical deposition (ECD) and atomic layer deposition (ALD). Wikipedia

Figure 7: Output for company description of Lam Research (Source: ChatGPT)

Using the 16 year old prompt

Think of Lam Research (ticker LRCX) like a high-tech "toolmaker" for the companies that build computer chips. Here's how it works, step by step:

1. **Chips are like really tiny cityscapes**
   - A semiconductor chip is built layer by layer on a flat piece of silicon, kind of like building roads, buildings, and bridges on a miniature city.
   - Each layer needs different materials (metals, insulators) and super-precise patterns.
2. **Lam makes the "construction machines"**
   - Just like you'd use a crane to lift steel or a concrete mixer to pour cement, chip makers use Lam's machines to deposit, etch, and clean these microscopic layers.
   - **Deposition tools** lay down thin films of material (imagine spray-painting a super-thin coat of paint, but at the atomic level).
   - **Etch tools** carve out patterns (like microscopic bulldozers cutting roads into that paint).
   - **Clean/strip tools** wash away leftovers so the next layer is spotless (like pressure-washing a surface between coats).

Figure 8: Output for company description of Lam Research with prompting (Source: ChatGPT)

Why does the "16-year-old prompt" work so well? Because it forces the AI to strip out jargon. If the tool can't explain a company simply enough for a first-day business student, you don't understand it well enough to risk real money on LEAPS.

There's no shame in sticking to businesses you can easily comprehend. Some of the best LEAPS opportunities are in companies with straightforward business models.

Building Your AI Research Assistant

Once you have a list of companies that you understand (and there is no harm in focusing on the bigger ones like Google), now we can add fuel to the fire.

We will have AI be our research assistant, so we will tell it

The output we want - specific analysis formats and conclusions

The sources we want it to use - earnings transcripts, SEC filings, analyst reports

What things are important to us, and what are not - LEAPS-specific factors versus day trading concerns

This is where your choice of AI tool becomes key, because not all AI tools will use the same datasets or sources.

Why Perplexity Beats ChatGPT for Financials

For financial analysis, I have found Perplexity AI to be the best performer. This is because it has access to earnings transcripts and SEC filings - the primary sources that matter for fundamental analysis.

ChatGPT and Claude are excellent for general analysis, but they often lack access to the most recent financial data. Perplexity can pull directly from company filings, recent earnings calls, and analyst reports to give you current, relevant information.

> Note: Perplexity is free for limited use - you get 3 "research" level searches per day, which is enough when starting out.

The Three-Prompt Research System That Replaces Hours of Work

Here's my exact system for researching LEAPS candidates using AI

Prompt 1: Core understanding

This prompt does the heavy lifting, we tell it the exact criteria we want to measure the business on, as well as the type of data we want the AI to use.

You are an equity research analyst specializing in providing unbiased analysis of public market companies. You search for the truth, weeding out the subjective from the objective.

You use the maximum amount of information available to you in your research, with a particular focus on SEC filings like the 10k and 10q, as well as quarterly earnings transcripts.

I need your help in analyzing and understanding a company and I want to know if it's a good investment opportunity or not - based on these 10 criteria

◇ Can I easily understand the business?

◇ Can it weather a storm? (Includes financial resilience, low debt, recurring revenue, and customer concentration risk)

◇ Is the industry growing or stable?

◇ Does the company have high lifetime customer value (LTV)? (Measured through unit economics, stickiness, pricing power, and industry-specific metrics like retention rate, customer ascension numbers and DBNRR for SaaS companies)

◇ Is there an intangible asset advantage? (Brand value, network effects, patents)

◇ Is there a moat? (High switching costs, pricing power, mass distribution)

42

◇ Does it have strong management? (measured by tenure, achievements, track record of stock appreciation)

◇ Is there significant insider ownership by management? (Anything above 10% is excellent)

◇ Are the key metrics improving? (Specific business KPIs like DAUs for tech, iPhone sales for Apple, % of subscribers upgrading for SaaS)

◇ Is there a healthy cash position? (more cash than debt, low debt levels in general, share buybacks)

Are you ready to assist me?

Once Perplexity confirms this, you can ask it to analyze the company of your choice. Then once that is done you will have an in-depth output and you can move on to prompt #2

Prompt 2: Scoring System

This prompt gives you a quantifiable score for each stock. Which is useful if you're trying to compare candidates.

"Now I want you to score the business on a scale of 1-100 using the above criteria, present the overall score at the end with a criteria of

STRONG BUY >80

BUY >70-79

WAIT >60-69

AVOID < 50-59

GARBAGE TIER < 50"

For context, here are several scores as of August 2025

◇ Nvidia - 91

◇ Mercado Libre - 85

◇ Google - 81

◇ Lam Research - 76

◇ Coreweave - 69

◇ Asana - 61

Prompt 3: Go or wait

In this final prompt, we will see if there are any last minute red flags that means we should wait, or if this stock is good to go.

"Now I want you to present the bear case. Why would the bull thesis fall apart? And score the risk factors on a scale of 1-10.

A risk score of <5 is PROCEED, 5.0-5.9 is PROCEED WITH CAUTION, anything above 6.0 should be listed as WAIT AND REASSESS"

This is important because you don't want to run into potential fundamental hurdles early in the trade. For example, here was the summary when I used this prompt for Google

"While our bull analysis scored Google at 81/100 for a STRONG BUY, the bear case reveals 6 out of 10 major risks scoring above 6.0, warranting a WAIT AND REASSESS recommendation with an average risk score of 6.4/10."

The AI noted the unsolved DOJ Antitrust breakup risk, and loss of revenue from the Apple search agreement as the being 2 key risk factors. And I agree. Until we get more clarity on that, I wouldn't want to enter a trade on GOOG.

But if you get a score of below 5, then you can definitely use that stock as a LEAPS candidate.

The 15-Minute Research Session

With practice, you can complete a thorough LEAPS research session in 15 minutes:

Minutes 1-3: Run the company through your understanding test

Minutes 4-12: Execute the three-prompt system in Perplexity

Minutes 13-15: Make go/no-go decision and add to watchlist or research queue

This systematic approach ensures you're making data-driven decisions rather than getting caught up in stories or momentum.

The goal isn't to become an expert on every company, instead it's to quickly identify which companies deserve deeper analysis and which ones you should avoid entirely. AI makes this process faster and more thorough than traditional research methods, but only if you use it correctly.

Why This Matters More Than Technical Analysis

I'm not dismissing technical analysis - timing matters for LEAPS entries. But over 12-24 months, fundamentals determine your success far more than chart patterns or momentum indicators.

The market loves a good story in the short term, but the numbers decide everything over longer time horizons. Companies with deteriorating fundamentals might rally for weeks or months, but they eventually disappoint. Companies with improving fundamentals might consolidate or even decline initially, but they tend to reward patient investors.

LEAPS give you the time to be right about the business, even if you're early on the timing.

There's one final part of this that we haven't touched on, namely valuation. We'll get into that in our next chapter.

Key Takeaways

◇ **First Principle of AI**: Garbage in, garbage out. Prompts matter over everything else.

◇ Don't buy LEAPS if you don't understand the company.

◇ AI tools (esp. Perplexity) can compress hours of research into minutes.

◇ **Three-Prompt System**:

　◇ Core analysis (10 fundamentals: moat, cash, LTV, insider ownership, etc.).

　◇ Scoring system (Strong Buy >80, Avoid <60).

　◇ Bear case & risk scoring.

◇ Use AI to screen quickly, but fundamentals must confirm.

Chapter 5

THE VALUATION EQUATION

After spending all that time researching fundamentals and understanding business models, many LEAPS traders make a critical error: they buy good companies at bad prices.

I learned this lesson the hard way in early 2021. I'd done my homework on a cloud software company - strong recurring revenue, expanding margins, dominant market position, everything you'd want in a LEAPS candidate. The fundamentals were pristine, my research confirmed my thesis, and I was convinced this was a winner.

There was just one problem, I was paying 80 times forward earnings for a company growing at 20% annually. The math didn't work, but I was so focused on the so-called quality of the business that I ignored the price I was paying for it.

Six months later, the stock had dropped 40% despite matching earnings estimates. The business was performing exactly as expected, but the market decided that 80x earnings was too expensive, even for what I believed was a great company.

That's when I realized that valuation isn't just important for LEAPS - it's often the determining factor between success and failure.

Why Valuation Matters More for LEAPS

With short-term options, you might get away with overpaying if momentum carries the stock higher quickly. But LEAPS give you 12-24 months for your investment to play out, and over that timeframe, valuation becomes a key arbiter of returns.

Here's the uncomfortable truth, while valuation doesn't matter much in the next two weeks, it matters enormously over 18-24 months. A high valuation ratio might be justified by growth expectations, but if that growth doesn't materialize, or if market sentiment shifts, expensive stocks get punished.

This is especially true in changing interest rate environments. When rates rise, investors become less willing to pay premium multiples for future growth. The stocks that get hit hardest are those trading at the highest valuations, regardless of business quality.

So when it comes to valuation, the majority of investors either skip it altogether, or one rely on one single metric - usually the Price to Earnings (PE) ratio. However, the PE ratio is one of the most misleading metrics in all of investing. Here's why that's the case...

The Tale of Two "Expensive" Stocks

Let me show you what I mean with two real examples from my research. The figures are correct as of August 2025.

Nike (NKE):

◇ Forward P/E: 44x (well above S&P 500 average of ~21x)

◇ EPS growth forecast: ~6% annually

Nvidia (NVDA):

◇ Forward P/E: 37x (also well above market average)

◇ EPS growth forecast: ~25% annually

Now on the surface, both Nike and Nvidia seem "overvalued" compared to the market average. But that's only surface level, and as I hope you'll have seen so far, that doesn't cut it in these parts.

If we look at the growth rates for both companies, Nvidia is projecting earnings growth at 5x the rate of Nike, and it doesn't take a genius to figure out that you can get away with paying more for a faster growing company.

Fortunately, we have a metric that factors this in. Whether Peter Lynch invented the Price-to-Earnings Growth (PEG) ratio or not, he certainly popularized it.

The PEG ratio is where you divide the PE by the earnings growth rate, to get a more accurate picture of the company's value in relation to its future prospects.

So while both companies had high P/E ratios, the PEG ratio told the real story.

◇ Nike - 44x forward P/E with 6% growth, gives us a PEG of just over 7

◇ Nvidia - 37x forward P/E with 25% growth, gives us a PEG of around 1.3

So now we see that Nike is "expensive" with little growth to justify the premium. Nvidia on the hand may be "expensive" but it at least has the growth profile to potentially support its valuation.

The lesson here - don't take PE ratos at face value, and PEG is a far better metric to use.

Valuation Guardrails (Mandatory Metrics)

Based on analyzing hundreds of LEAPS trades, I've developed some valuation guardrails that every position must meet

PEG ratio (forward) ≤ 1.5 as the default rule-of-thumb. This normalizes valuation for growth and prevents you from overpaying for slow-growing companies.

Forward P/E compared to the company's 5-year average. If today's forward P/E is lower, that's usually a green light. If it's higher, make sure growth is accelerating enough to justify it. Higher than average + slowing growth is a red flag whereas higher than average + accelerating growth can be a valid reason to pay up.

Share dilution ≤ 3% per year over the past 3 years. Excessive dilution quietly erodes shareholder returns even if the business performs well.

This workflow is a beginner-friendly system. There are more advanced ways to value companies (DCF models, EV/EBITDA, sum-of-parts, etc.), but those belong in a more advanced book. For LEAPS beginners, PEG and P/E vs history are more than enough to avoid overpaying.

Valuation Tools & Process

The beauty of modern valuation analysis is that you don't need complex models or expensive software. You only need a stock screener and five minutes per company.

Here's my exact process using StockAnalysis

Step 1: Type in the ticker symbol

Step 2: Record three key metrics (you can find these in the statistics tab)

◇ Forward P/E ratio

◇ PEG ratio

◇ 3-year share count change

Step 3: Compare each metric to the company's historical multiples

Step 4: Focus on PEG to normalize valuation for growth

Step 5: Only proceed if valuation is fair or slightly above average with clear growth acceleration

This entire process takes less than five minutes per company and eliminates most valuation mistakes before they happen.

Common Valuation Mistakes in LEAPS

Treating all high P/Es as equally bad without adjusting for growth rates - A 30x P/E on 25% growth is very different from 30x P/E on 5% growth.

Using trailing P/E instead of forward P/E - LEAPS are forward-looking instruments, so you need forward-looking valuations.

Ignoring share dilution - A company can grow earnings while destroying per-share value through excessive stock issuance.

Entering at all-time-high multiples without evidence of growth acceleration - If a company has never traded at these valuations before, there must be a compelling reason why now is different.

One-Page Valuation Workflow

Here's the exact checklist I use for every LEAPS candidate:

Step 1: Open your preferred screener and enter the ticker

Step 2: Record the three mandatory metrics:

◇ Forward P/E: ＿＿

◇ Forward PEG: ＿＿

◇ 3-year share dilution: ＿＿%

Step 3: Compare to benchmarks:

◇ Company's 5-year average P/E: ＿＿

◇ Sector median P/E: ＿＿

◇ Market average P/E: ~21x

Step 4: Ask the critical question: "Is PEG ≤ 1.5?" If not, is there a credible reason for paying up?

Step 5: Make the decision: Only proceed if valuation is fair or slightly above average with clear growth acceleration.

This workflow takes less than five minutes but prevents most valuation-related losses.

When to Pay Up for Quality

There are times when paying a premium multiple makes sense for LEAPS:

Accelerating growth: If a company's growth rate is increasing, higher multiples may be justified

Market leadership: Dominant companies in growing markets often deserve premium valuations

Margin expansion: Companies improving profitability can support higher multiples

Capital efficiency: Businesses with high returns on invested capital earn premium valuations over time

The key is having evidence that the premium is justified by improving fundamentals, not just hoping that expensive stocks will get more expensive.

The Valuation Safety Net

Remember, valuation acts as your safety net in LEAPS investing. Even if your fundamental thesis is wrong, buying at reasonable valuations limits your downside. Conversely, even if your fundamental analysis is perfect, overpaying can turn a great business into a poor investment.

The most successful LEAPS traders I know aren't necessarily the best at picking businesses - they're the most disciplined about the prices they pay for those businesses.

In the next chapter, we'll explore how to structure your LEAPS positions for maximum profit potential while controlling risk. Because once you've identified a fundamentally sound company at a reasonable valuation, the way you structure the trade determines whether you capture the full upside or leave money on the table.

Key Takeaways

◇ Many lose money by buying great companies at bad prices.

◇ Valuation matters more over 18–24 months than in short-term trading.

◇ PEG ratio (PE ÷ growth rate) is superior to plain PE.

◇ Guardrails:

◇ PEG ≤ 1.5.

◇ Forward PE vs 5-yr average.

◇ Share dilution ≤ 3%.

◇ Avoid common mistakes: trailing PEs, ignoring dilution, paying peak multiples.

◇ Valuation is your safety net in LEAPS.

Chapter 6

BUILDING THE LEAPS TRADE

I was staring at my screen on a Tuesday morning in March, watching a stock I'd been researching for months (TTD) finally hit my target entry price. The fundamentals were solid, the valuation was reasonable, and the technical setup looked perfect. Everything was aligned for what could be a great LEAPS trade.

But instead of jumping in immediately like I used to do, I opened OptionStrat and started modeling the trade. I wanted to see exactly how much I could lose if my support level broke, and if you remember what happened in April, that stock, like many others, saw it's support level get crushed on the tariff announcements.

What I realized was the difference between a haphazard entry and a systematically planned trade isn't just better risk management - it's often the difference between a 50% gain and a 200% gain on the same underlying move.

That disciplined approach to trade construction has become the foundation of every LEAPS position I take.

Step 1: Confirm the Thesis Window

Before you even look at option chains, you need to match your expiration date to your investment thesis timeline. This sounds obvious, but most traders get it backwards - they pick an expiration based on price rather than probability.

Rule: LEAPS expiry should match the time you expect your thesis to play out.

Default: 18-24 months from entry date.

Here's why this matters: if you believe a company's turnaround will take 18 months to show results, buying a 12-month LEAPS creates unnecessary time pressure. Conversely, if you expect a catalyst within 18 months, paying for 36 months of time premium is wasteful.

Longer expirations give you room for volatility and unexpected delays. Shorter expirations risk having your thesis proven right after your option expires worthless.

Also note that certain lower volume stocks won't have as many different LEAPS expiration dates as higher volume ones. For example, Nvidia currently has 6 expiration dates more than 1 year out, whereas a lower volume stock like TTD only has 2.

Step 2: Strike Selection

This is where most LEAPS traders make their biggest mistake. They buy cheap, out-of-the-money (OTM) calls hoping for lottery ticket returns, then wonder why small stock moves don't translate into option profits.

Target Delta: 0.80-0.90 for stock-like behavior.

This usually means strikes that are 10-20% in-the-money. Yes, they cost more upfront, but they move almost dollar-for-dollar with the underlying stock. When you're right about direction, you capture most of the move.

Avoid far out-of-the-money strikes for long-term trades. A 0.30 delta option needs the stock to move significantly just to break even.

Here's the math behind this strategy using NVDA.

I'm using the Jun 2027 expiry - which at the time of writing is 671 days away, and for reference Nvidia is trading at $182.

The 130 strike (80 delta) has a $74.25 premium

Breakeven stock price for the trade to be profitable = (strike + premium paid) = (130 + 74.25) = $204.25

Now let's compare this to an OTM call at the same expiry date

The 290 strike (30 delta) has a $27.65 premium

Breakeven stock price = (290 + 27.65) = $317.65

So while the OTM call may be cheaper, you need the stock to appreciate 50% more for the trade to be profitable. Remember that LEAPS are best used as a synthetic stock replacement rather than a speculative tool.

Step 3: Using OptionStrat

The free trade builder tool at OptionStrat.com is essential for proper LEAPS construction. Here's my exact process. You can find a video walkthrough of this in the bonus section at freemanpublications.com/bonus

Build Trade → Long Call

Select your target expiry (18-24 months) and strike (closest to delta 0.80-0.90).

Use the price slider to find the option value if the stock drops to your identified support level. This number becomes your maximum dollar risk per contract, meaning the potential loss from entry price down to your stop-loss, not the full premium you paid.

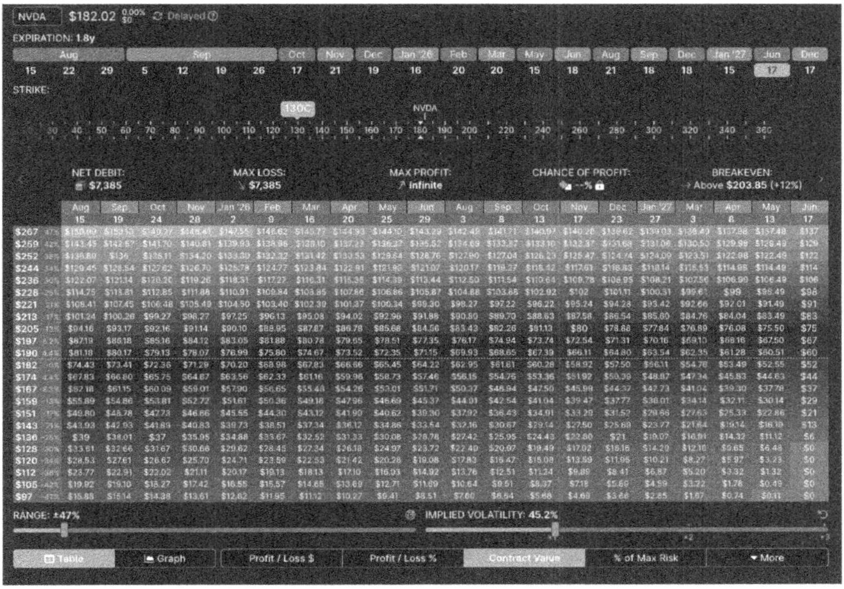

Figure 9: NVDA LEAPS Profit level (Source: Optionstrat.com)

Compare to your 5% Max Dollar Risk Table: Your total portfolio value × 5% ÷ per-contract risk = maximum contracts allowed.

This modeling takes 2 minutes but prevents position sizing mistakes that can destroy your account.

Step 4: Stop-Loss & Support

Your stop-loss should be based on technical levels, not arbitrary percentages. Use moving averages to identify where your thesis would be invalidated.

Place your stop just below support to avoid whipsaws from normal market noise. For example, if Nvidia shows support at $143, I'll put my stop just below, say at $140. Why not right on the line? Because if you set it exactly at support, you risk getting shaken out by normal volatility. By placing it just under, you give the trade breathing room while still protecting your capital if the thesis breaks.

The option value at this price level equals your dollar risk per contract. If you can't accept this loss, don't take the trade.

Support levels provide a logical line in the sand. If a stock breaks below major support, something fundamental may have changed about your thesis.

Step 5: Position Sizing

This is non-negotiable: never risk more than 5% of your total portfolio on any single LEAPS trade.

5% Max Risk Rule: Portfolio × 5% ÷ per-contract risk = contracts allowed.

Never size based on "affordability" - only risk tolerance. Just because you can afford 10 contracts doesn't mean you should buy them if it violates your risk management rules.

Case Study: Nvidia (NVDA)

Let me walk you through exactly how I would structure a LEAPS trade on Nvidia using this framework:

Thesis: Market leader in AI computing with CUDA software moat and GPU dominance. Strong growth runway from AI adoption across industries.

Fundamentals:

◇ Fundamental analysis score: 91 (STRONG BUY)

◇ Risk score: 4.6/10 (PROCEED)

◇ Revenue growth forecast: ~25% annually

◇ EPS growth forecast: ~25% annually

◇ ROE: > 60%

◇ Indicates above average profitability and efficiency compared to industry peers

◇ Net cash position

◇ Share dilution: < 1% annually

Valuation:

◇ Forward P/E: 37× (market average ~21×)

◇ Forward PEG: ~1.3 → Premium justified by growth

◇ Slightly above 5-year average but growth accelerating

Chart Analysis:

◇ Key support: $143 (previous breakout level, now new support)

◇ Secondary support: 200-day moving average at $137

◇ Currently consolidating above $145 post-earnings

◇ Volume patterns show institutional accumulation

OptionStrat Setup:

◇ Expiry: 20 months out (Jun 17, 2027)

◇ Strike: $130 (delta ~0.80, about 20% in-the-money)

◇ Option price: ~$74 ($7,400 per contract)

◇ Take profit: 100% gain on initial options contract (option price $148)

◇ Depending on the timeframe, this would be a 45-55% gain in the stock price (between $257-277 per share)

◇ Stop-loss: If stock breaks $140 → option value drops to ~$41

◇ Max dollar risk: $3,200 per contract ($7,400 - $4,100)

Portfolio Sizing:

◇ Max risk allowed: $3,200 (5% rule)

◇ Minimum Portfolio size to do this trade = (3,200 * 20) = $64,000

Risk Management:

◇ Stop-loss at $140 (clear technical level)

◇ Position size keeps total risk under 5% of portfolio

◇ 20-month expiration provides ample time for thesis to play out

If you've filled out your trade plan, and calculated the above numbers - you can go ahead and confidently enter the trade! In the next chapter we'll cover how to monitor the trade, and adjust it if necessary, so you can maximize your chance of profiting.

Key Takeaways

◇ Match expiration to thesis window (18–24 months typical).

◇ Strike selection: Use 0.80–0.90 delta ITM calls to mimic stock-like behavior.

◇ Avoid cheap OTM "lottery ticket" LEAPS.

◇ OptionStrat modeling defines dollar risk & stop-loss.

◇ Position sizing must follow the 5% portfolio rule.

Chapter 7

WHAT TO DO WHEN THINGS DO (OR DON'T) GO WRONG

I've been investing for 16 years now, and since I bought my first stock (McDonald's) in 2008, there's one thing that continues to frustrate me to this day. When I buy a stock and it goes straight down.

Sometimes, no matter how much research you do, or no matter how good the chart looks, Mr. Market works against you. My old reaction to this would be to curse various deities for being against me, and rant to my girlfriend (now wife) about how the market isn't fair.

But over the past 5 years I've developed a better approach, one which has helped both my portfolio returns, and my sanity.

Before I get into the framework around adjusting your trade, I want to make one thing abundantly clear. Whether you're buying and holding a stock, or buying LEAPS, there is no perfect adjustment system or strategy that turns every losing position into a winner. If there were, I'd probably be typing this from a megayacht or on a private island named after me.

What we do have though is a rules-based system that allows you to always have an answer for "what-should-I-do-right-now" - that's what we'll discuss in this chapter.

Why Adjustments Matter

LEAPS span years, which means stocks will cycle through rallies, drifts, and pullbacks. Without adjustments, you risk having positions expire too soon before your thesis plays out, or lose delta if contracts drift too far ITM or OTM.

Here's the key insight, in the first 6-12 months, LEAPS lose very little time value. You rarely need to make snap decisions, meaning patience itself is the first "adjustment."

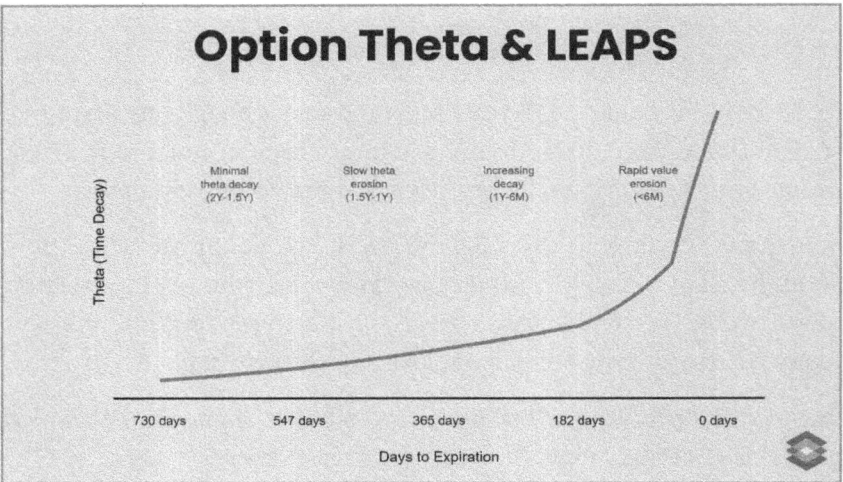

Figure 10: Theta decay for 2 year LEAPS (Source: tradingblock.com)

This contrasts sharply with short-term options that demand adjustments "right now." LEAPS allow structured, deliberate decisions made over weeks or months, not minutes or hours.

Scenario 0: Patience (Default State)

I cannot stress this enough, most trades require no adjustment early on. If your stock dips but remains above long-term support, simply wait. Check in monthly, not daily. Your first adjustment is often just holding your nerve, and trust me when I say you will lose more money trying to overcorrect trades early, than you will just by sitting on your hands and letting time run it's course.

This is harder than it sounds because if you see a position down 10% after two months, every instinct tells you to "do something." But LEAPS are designed for exactly these situations - temporary setbacks that resolve over time.

Scenario 1: Trade Working (Stock Up, LEAPS Profitable)

The problem with winning trades is that deep in-the-money contracts lose leverage as delta approaches 1. At that point your option moves dollar-for-dollar with the stock, great in absolute terms, but it erases the percentage advantage of LEAPS.

Here's why: say you bought a call for $80 when the stock was $150. Now the stock has run to $200, your option is worth $120 and delta is 1. A further $1 rise adds $1 to the option, but $1 on $120 is less than 1%. Compare that to earlier, when the same $1 move added $1 on an $80 option, a 1.25% jump.

In other words, your leverage fades as delta climbs, which is why we often "roll up" into a new 0.80 delta LEAPS call. This is because it resets the leverage, locks in profits, and reduces capital at risk.

So the standard adjustment here is to roll out and up - extend the expiry another 12 months and reset the strike higher to maintain approximately 0.80 delta. This allows you to bank some profits, reduce capital at risk, and keep your thesis alive with proper leverage.

Scenario 2: Trade Neutral (Stock Sideways, LEAPS Stagnant)

When stocks consolidate for months, theta begins nibbling at your position slowly. The stock isn't moving against you, but time is passing and your option isn't gaining value.

The adjustment is to roll out while keeping the same strike. This adds time and resets the clock so your thesis can still play out. You're essentially buying more runway for your idea to work.

Scenario 3: Trade Not Working (Stock Down, LEAPS Losing Value)

This is the most challenging scenario. Your position is bleeding value and delta is dropping below 0.70, reducing your participation in any potential recovery.

You have two main options: roll down and out to reset closer to the current stock price and restore approximately 0.80 delta, or exit the trade entirely if the fundamentals have changed.

There's also an assignment consideration: if it's a stock you'd happily own long-term, you can let the LEAPS expire into shares at expiry. But remember - never exercise early, as you'll lose time value. Always sell-to-close or roll until expiry.

Mechanics of Rolling

Timing is crucial - you want to roll around 90 days to expiration or when delta drifts too far from your target range. The process involves closing your old contract and opening a new one further out, typically resetting delta to approximately 0.80.

Always ensure you roll your LEAPS with more than 60 DTE, otherwise you'll see the time value of your initial trade fall off a cliff, and you'll have to pay more to roll as a result. So between 60 and 90 DTE is the sweet spot.

Use OptionStrat to compare the old versus new payoff profiles before making any moves. This helps you understand exactly what you're gaining and giving up with each adjustment.

From a capital management perspective, rolling up allows you to lock in profits while maintaining exposure. Rolling down adds cost to your position, so make sure it fits within your 5% portfolio risk rule.

Case Studies

Banking GOOG profits

Let's say you entered a LEAPS in January 2024 position with a $100 strike call (80 delta), 619 days to expiration, costing $49.90.

As the stock moved from $136 to $204 over the next 18 months, the option value increased to $104.35 due to huge jump in intrinsic value, and is now at a 97 delta.

You want to bank some profits, but keep the trade open as you believe Google still has more room to run. You can roll up and out, pushing your expiry date back another 16 months to December 2026.

To do this, you sell your initial call for $104.35, and open a new trade at the 150 strike (80 delta). This new option costs $67.90.

Your total outlay at this point is just $1,346 to effectively control 80 shares of Google.

If you're wondering how I got that number it's

The initial premium you paid (-$49.90) plus the sale of the initial call ($104.35) minus the new call (-$67.90)

By moving to higher strike, you lock in part of your profits and resetting the delta while banking gains. This reduces your capital at risk while extending time for the thesis to continue working.

The outcome was gains banked, risk reduced, and time extended - exactly what a successful roll should accomplish.

Nvidia (NVDA) - Roll Out, Same Strike

I had entered with a $130 strike call, 24 months out, with delta around 0.85. The stock consolidated around $145 for nine months, causing delta to drop to 0.70 while the option stagnated.

The adjustment was rolling out 12 months at the same strike, which extended time and kept the thesis alive until the next AI-driven rally materialized.

This type of roll is pure time extension - you're not changing your bet, just giving it more runway to work.

Writing Your Adjustment Playbook

Before entering any LEAPS position, pre-plan your decisions:

If the stock rallies strongly, you'll roll out and up to maintain leverage while banking profits.

If it moves sideways for 12+ months, you'll roll out at the same strike to extend time.

If the stock drops significantly, you'll either roll down and out to restore delta, or exit if fundamentals have deteriorated - remember you would have set this up using your stop loss when you initially entered the trade.

If you'd be happy owning the stock long-term, you might let it expire into assignment rather than rolling.

The hard rule that applies to all scenarios: never exercise early. Always sell or roll until expiry to preserve time value.

Key Takeaways

◇ Default adjustment = patience (most trades don't need immediate fixes).

◇ Adjustment scenarios:

◇ Stock Up: Roll out + up to lock profits, reset delta.

◇ Stock Sideways: Roll out, same strike to add time.

◇ Stock Down: Roll down + out, or exit if fundamentals break.

◇ Mechanics: Roll 60–90 DTE before expiry.

◇ Build a written adjustment playbook before entering trades.

Chapter 8

THE SMART MAN'S COVERED CALL - GENERATING INCOME WHILE YOU WAIT

Here's a problem every investor faces - you've done your research, found a great company, bought the perfect LEAPS position, and now you're waiting 12-18 months for your thesis to play out. Your position might be profitable, but it's just sitting there, not generating any cash flow while you wait.

Meanwhile, you're watching other investors collect monthly income from covered calls on stocks like Apple and Microsoft. The problem is you don't have an extra $20,000 to buy 100 shares of Apple, or $50,000 for Microsoft. So you're locked out of these income strategies because of capital requirements.

The solution is the Smart Man's Covered Call (SMCC) - a strategy that lets you generate monthly income from pricier stocks using your LEAPS position as collateral instead of owning the actual shares.

This is usually known as the Poor Man's Covered Call (PMCC), but I've always thought it was a stupid name, and my good friend Anthony came up with SMCC as the superior moniker, so that's what we'll use in the remainder of this book.

With the SMCC, you get nearly identical economics to a traditional covered call, but with 50-80% less capital required.

What is a Smart Man's Covered Call?

To understand SMCCs, you first need to understand traditional covered calls. A covered call involves owning 100 shares of stock and selling a call option against those shares. The stock provides the underlying exposure you want, while the short call generates monthly income. If the call gets exercised, you simply deliver your shares at the strike price.

A SMCC combines two positions: a long LEAPS call and a short-term call sold against it. Instead of owning 100 shares plus selling a call, you have a LEAPS call and a a shorter-term call.

Your LEAPS call acts as the "stock" position, providing the underlying exposure, while the short call generates income.

The key is structure, your LEAPS should be deep ITM with a high delta (0.80-0.90) and long expiration (12+ months remaining), while your short call should be OTM with a low delta (0.20-0.30) and short expiration (30-45 days).

Why SMCCs Work So Well with LEAPS

LEAPS are perfect for SMCCs because they behave like stock ownership with several advantages:

Capital efficiency - Control 100 shares for a fraction of the cost of buying them outright

Time stability - Your long option loses value slowly, while your short option decays quickly in your favor

Delta differential - High delta LEAPS move almost 1:1 with the stock, while low delta short calls move much less

Flexibility - Can close the short call anytime without affecting your underlying LEAPS position

The strategy works because you're long time (LEAPS) and short time (weekly/monthly calls). Time decay hurts your LEAPS minimally but helps your short calls significantly.

Setting Up the SMCC

Step 1: LEAPS Selection

◇ Minimum 12 months to expiration (preferably 18-24)

◇ Delta 0.80-0.90 (deep in-the-money for stock-like behavior)

◇ Liquid options with tight bid-ask spreads

Why Liquidity Matters in SMCCs

Liquidity isn't just a technical detail - it's often the difference between executing your strategy smoothly and getting trapped in positions you can't exit when you need to.

Before entering any Smart Man's Covered Call, check these liquidity metrics to ensure you can get in and out at fair prices:

Open Interest: Look for at least 100 contracts of open interest at your target strike and expiration. This indicates sufficient market participation to support reasonable pricing.

Bid-Ask Spread: Avoid options with spreads wider than $0.50 on contracts worth $10 or more. Wide spreads represent hidden transaction costs that eat into your profits every time you enter or exit a position.

Exit Flexibility: Remember that illiquid LEAPS can leave you stuck in positions even when the underlying stock trades actively. Your ability to adjust or close positions depends entirely on options market liquidity, not stock liquidity.

The rule is simple - if the option chain looks sparse or inactive, find a different opportunity. Liquidity represents your exit door, so never enter a trade without confirming you can get out when your strategy demands it.

Step 2: Short Call Selection

◇ 30-45 days to expiration

◇ Delta 0.20-0.30 (out-of-the-money for income generation)

◇ Strike price <u>above</u> your LEAPS break-even point

Step 3: Timing

◇ Avoid earnings weeks unless you want the extra volatility

◇ Consider technical resistance levels for short strike selection

Managing the SMCC

Profit Taking: Close short calls at 50-80% profit rather than holding to expiration. This frees up capital for the next cycle and reduces assignment risk.

Rolling: If the short call moves in-the-money, you can roll it out and up to collect additional premium while avoiding assignment.

Assignment Management: If assigned, you'll deliver your LEAPS instead of stock. This effectively closes your entire position, so only accept assignment if you're ready to exit.

Case Study: Palo Alto Networks SMCC

Let me walk through a detailed PANW trade that shows exactly how this strategy works.

Initial Setup

PANW is trading at $180. My 30,000 foot thesis for a LEAPS position was the company's increasing dominance as a platform provider in cybersecurity, moving customers away from the individual solution approach. The company was still growing revenue in the mid-teens despite now being at a $9.5B annual run rate, all while expanding margins (note: this was before the CyberArk acquisition - which further strengthened my thesis)

So here was the trade.

◇ Bought 21-month LEAPS: $130 strike, delta 0.81, cost $6,875

◇ Sold first short call: $200 strike, 30 DTE, delta 0.28, collected $265

Month 1: Stock flat, short call expired

Month 2: Sold $200 call, 30 days out, collected $280. Stock rallied to $202, rolled call up and out for another 30 days to the $205 strike for $80 credit - Net: $525 (265+280+80)

Month 3: Stock moves slightly upwards nearing $205 strike, rolled call up and out to $210 strike for another 30 days for a $105 credit - Net: $630 (265+280+80+105)

Month 4: Stock pulls back to $202 - $210 strike expires worthless

Total Results:

◇ LEAPS appreciation: $1,200 (stock moved from $180 to $192)

◇ Premium collected: $630 over 4 months

◇ Total return: $1,200 in unrealized gains, $630 in realized gains

◇ $630 made on $6,875 of capital = 9.1% in 4 months (27.3% annualized)

So as you can see here, adding in the SMCC made me an extra $630 - not bad for an hour's work.

Income Expectations

When setting up SMCCs, you can realistically expect monthly income ranging from 1-3% of your LEAPS value. This range depends heavily on several key factors that determine how much premium you can collect.

Volatility levels play the biggest role in determining your income potential. Higher implied volatility (IV) means more premium to collect from your short calls, while low volatility environments offer fewer income opportunities. Strike selection creates a constant trade-off between income and risk - selling calls closer to the current stock price generates more premium but increases your chances of assignment.

Market conditions also influence your results significantly. Trending markets often provide better premium opportunities as investors are willing to pay more for protection or speculation.

The key is not to chase unrealistic income targets that force you into high-risk situations. Consistent 1-2% monthly returns compound to excellent annual performance while keeping risk manageable. Remember, you're already getting leveraged exposure to stock appreciation through your LEAPS - so the income from SMCCs is a bonus, not the primary objective.

Common SMCC Mistakes

The most costly mistake is using LEAPS with too little time remaining. Once you're inside 12 months to expiration, theta acceleration makes the strategy less effective as your long option starts losing value more rapidly. This erodes the time advantage that makes SMCCs work.

Many traders also sell calls too close to the money in pursuit of higher premiums. This creates constant assignment risk that defeats the entire purpose of capital efficiency. You'll spend more time managing the position and face frequent early closures that reduce overall profitability.

Another critical error is ignoring your LEAPS break-even point when selecting short strikes. Like with a regular covered call, avoid selling calls below your total cost basis, as this locks in losses if you get assigned. Your short strike should always be <u>above</u> the price where your entire position becomes profitable. You also have to be aware of earnings, which can create big volatility spikes that work against you. While elevated volatility increases premium collection, it also increases the likelihood of large stock moves that could result in assignment or force you to close positions at unfavorable prices.

> Special note on earnings: I generally avoid selling short calls right into earnings week. Premiums are fat, but so is the risk of a big move that forces you to buy back at a loss. Unless I specifically want that risk, I'll skip that cycle and sell again after earnings.

When SMCCs Don't Work

Strongly trending stocks present your biggest challenge through constant assignment risk. If a stock keeps rallying month after month, you'll find yourself repeatedly buying back short calls at losses or getting assigned out of positions before your long-term thesis can fully play out. This is the antithesis of why you'd even enter a LEAPS position in the first place.

More importantly than that, SMCCs don't work if you lack the time for proper management. The strategy requires 15-30 minutes a month to roll positions, monitor assignment risk, and optimize strike selection. If you can't dedicate this time consistently, you're better off with simpler buy-and-hold LEAPS strategies.

> ### Author's Note
>
> I don't personally sell SMCCs on every LEAPS position. In fact, most of the time I don't.

The reason is simple: not every stock is suitable for this strategy. Fast-moving stocks like Nvidia or Nubank can turn a conservative SMCC into a high-stress trade overnight, forcing you to constantly manage assignment risk instead of letting your long-term thesis play out peacefully.

I reserve SMCCs for specific situations where the conditions align properly. The stock needs to be consolidating or trading sideways rather than trending strongly in either direction. I need to be genuinely comfortable exiting at the short strike price if assigned - this isn't a strategy for positions where I desperately want to hold for the full term and potentially take ownership of the stock. Finally, I want to generate extra income while waiting for a slower-developing thesis to unfold, particularly when I expect the catalyst to take 12-18 months to materialize.

Think of SMCCs as one tool in your toolkit, not a mandatory step in every LEAPS trade. The foundation of successful LEAPS investing remains long-term conviction in great businesses bought at reasonable prices. SMCCs are simply one way to enhance returns when the specific conditions make it appropriate, but they should never become the tail that wags the dog.

Your primary focus should always be on identifying and holding quality positions for the long term. The income strategies are secondary benefits that you can layer on when suitable, not requirements for every trade.

Risk Management

The maximum risk in a SMCC is straightforward to calculate as it's your LEAPS premium minus any short call premium you've collected. This amount is known upfront and doesn't change regardless of how the stock moves, giving you complete clarity on your potential loss before entering the trade.

Assignment risk exists but is manageable through careful strike selection and rolling techniques. Here's what many traders worry about: "What happens if my short call gets exercised and I have LEAPS instead of actual shares?" The answer is simpler than most people think.

When your short call gets assigned, your broker will automatically exercise your LEAPS to deliver the required shares to the call buyer. You don't need to own the actual stock - your LEAPS contract gives you the right to buy shares at the strike price, which your broker exercises to fulfill the assignment obligation. The entire process happens automatically, and you'll receive cash for the difference.

For example, if you own a $100 strike LEAPS and get assigned on a $120 short call, your broker exercises your LEAPS (buying shares at $100) and immediately sells them at $120 to satisfy the assignment. You keep the $20 per share difference, plus any premium you collected from selling the call.

Remember, assignment isn't necessarily bad - it just closes your position, potentially at a profit. If you get assigned above your break-even point, you've achieved exactly what you set out to do: profit from the stock's appreciation while collecting income along the way. The key is ensuring your short strike is always above your total cost basis so that assignment results in a gain, not a loss.

The real power of SMCCs becomes apparent over time. You're earning income while your LEAPS appreciates, creating a compound effect that can significantly outperform buy-and-hold strategies.

Consider a $50,000 portfolio running 5 SMCC positions, each generating 1.5% monthly income. That's $750 per month in additional cash flow, or $9,000 annually - an 18% yield on top of any capital appreciation from your LEAPS positions.

This income can be reinvested into new LEAPS positions, used to diversify into other strategies, or simply taken as cash flow for living expenses.

In the next chapter, we'll explore advanced LEAPS strategies that can further optimize your returns, including how to use LEAPS for portfolio hedging and sector rotation plays that institutional investors employ regularly.

Key Takeaways

◇ SMCC = LEAPS + short-term OTM call (instead of stock + call).

◇ Provides covered call-like income with 50–80% less capital.

   ◇ Setup: LEAPS (12–24 months, delta 0.80–0.90) + short call (30–45 DTE, delta 0.20–0.30).

◇ Manage by closing short calls at 50–80% profit and rolling if ITM.

◇ Expect 1–2% monthly income.

◇ Avoid mistakes: using short-dated LEAPS, selling calls too close to money, ignoring breakeven.

Chapter 9

USING LEAPS TO PROTECT YOUR PORTFOLIO

It's March 2020. The S&P 500 falls 34% in just over a month. Retirement accounts that took decades to build are down six figures in weeks. Panic is everywhere.

I wasn't worried about the end of capitalism (ok maybe a bit...) but I was concerned about my family's financial security. Deep down I knew that markets would recover, but I certainly didn't know how long it would take and I didn't fancy spending years digging out of a deep hole.

That's when I realized that hedging isn't about predicting crashes, it's about buying insurance. So you don't have to panic-sell when everyone else is losing their minds, or watch years of hard work unwind in a matter months. Just like my own grandfather did in 2008 when his advisor-led portfolio of bank stocks and telecom companies cratered during the Global Financial Crisis, wiping out 50 years of hard work.

Done right, hedging provides the peace of mind that lets you sleep when markets drop. It offers capital protection that reduces drawdowns, making it easier to stay invested when others are capitulating. That way you also get to benefit from a rebound, unlike those who sell everything and sit on the sidelines as the market grinds higher post bear market, I witnessed many such cases first hand in 2020 and 2022.

Before we dive deeper, I want to get clear on one thing though. I spend precisely zero time thinking about *why* a potential crash could occur. You don't get any bonus points for being right on that front. Instead I solely focus on making sure I have the right protection in place in case of a downturn, no matter the reasons for said downturn.

Think of hedging like insurance, you don't buy car insurance expecting a crash - you buy it so one event doesn't wipe you out financially. The same principle applies to your investment portfolio.

Why Using LEAPS Puts Beat "Traditional Hedging"

Traditional hedging approaches have failed spectacularly in recent years, leaving investors exposed when they needed protection most.

The cookie cutter advice has been to use bonds as a hedging tool, as in theory they should perform as an inverse of the stock market. Unfortunately, the data doesn't support this claim. In fact, the classic 60/40 portfolio of stocks and bonds collapsed in 2022 when both asset classes fell together - bonds dropped 13% while stocks fell 18%, destroying the fundamental assumption that bonds will always provide diversification during equity downturns.

Then we have newer innovations like Inverse ETFs (SH and PSQ being the most popular), which on the surface appear attractive as hedging vehicles. These products are designed to move opposite to their underlying index on a daily basis, but they suffer from daily reset mechanisms that cause structural decay when held long-term. So over weeks or months, the compounding effects of daily rebalancing erode their effectiveness. What looks like perfect negative correlation on paper becomes a slowly melting ice cube in practice.

Then we have the more DIY approach of diversifying into different sectors, especially "defensive" ones like utilities, consumer staples, and healthcare. However this rarely provides meaningful protection during broad market downturns.

In 2008, utilities fell 29% while the S&P 500 dropped 37% - hardly the protection investors expected. During the March 2020 crash, even defensive sectors like consumer staples fell 24% as the entire market sold off indiscriminately. The 2022 bear market saw similar patterns, with supposedly defensive sectors providing minimal cushioning against the broader decline. When fear takes hold, correlations approach 1.0 and sector diversification becomes largely meaningless.

However, there *is* a better approach. LEAPS index ETF puts on SPY, QQQ, or IWM offer efficient, cost-effective, broad protection that actually works when you need it most.

Here's an important note: the best time to implement a hedge is in normal market conditions, when volatility is low and everything feels calm. If you wait until a correction has already started, implied volatility spikes, and you'll often pay 50-150% more for the same hedge.

For example, with SPY trading around $645, a 386 DTE $570 put when VIX is 15 might cost around $1,800. That same contract when VIX is 30 would cost around $3,600. Like all insurance, hedges are cheapest when you least feel like you need them.

The Mechanics of a Hedge (Step-by-Step)

Step 1: Decide What to Protect

If your portfolio is 100% tech and AI stocks, then hedging using SPY is only going to give you some protection. Conversely if all you own is energy companies, hedging using QQQ won't work either. So first things first, see which major index your portfolio is most heavily correlated with. Many brokerages will tell you this, but you can also export your portfolio as a CSV file and ask a tool like Perplexity to calculate the number for you.

Here are the numbers for my long term portfolio (tech heavy with a few large positions in non-US growth stocks)

◇ Correlation with SPY - 0.888

◇ Correlation with QQQ - 0.923

◇ Correlation with IWM - 0.790

The rule is simple: hedge the index that best mirrors your portfolio risk. So if I were hedging my own portfolio, a QQQ hedge would give me the most protection, with an IWM hedge the least.

> Note: You'll notice I keep mentioning SPY, QQQ, and IWM rather than the raw indexes. That's because ETFs are easier to trade, have tighter spreads, and give you the choice of settling into cash or stock. Indexes like SPX are cash-settled only, which is fine for advanced traders, but for most beginners, ETFs like SPY are simpler.

Step 2: Choose the Put Contract

Select an expiry 12-18 months out with a strike slightly out-of-the-money, about 5% below the current price. Target a delta around 0.35-0.40, which provides meaningful protection without being overly expensive.

Do not hedge with shorter contracts (<90 DTE), the time decay will eat away at your option premium at a faster rate than the index will likely keep up with.

Step 3: Position Sizing

You want your hedge to cover the majority, if not all of your portfolio. So you want the $ value of your hedging put contracts (strike price * 100) to roughly equal the dollar value of your account.

So if you have a $300,000 portfolio, 5 contracts of SPY at a 620 strike provides $310,000 worth of hedged positions.

(620 * 100) * 5 = $310,000

If you hedge in the way recommended in this book, during normal market conditions, generally this will cost you 3-4% per year up front.

For a $500,000 portfolio, that means $10,000-$15,000 per year on hedge premiums. Remember, your hedge is not designed to provide massive gains, instead it's insurance. As part of this, you will slightly underperform in good years because of this.

Case Study: $1,000,000 Portfolio Hedge

Consider a $1,000,000 portfolio with 100% equity exposure, highly correlated with SPY.

Your hedge setup might involve buying 16 SPY puts, 15 months out, 5% out-of-the-money, with delta around 0.35.

At the time of writing, this would be the 615 strike, and 16 puts would provide protection for $984,000 or 98.4% of the portfolio.

The cost of these puts would be approximately $35,000, representing 3.5% of your total portfolio.

Here's how this setup would perform vs. non-hedged approach (numbers from Optionstrat.com)

	Buy & hold performance	Hedge portfolio performance
SPY +30%	+30%	+26.5%
SPY +10%	+10%	+6.5%
SPY flat	0%	-3.5%
SPY -10%	-10%	-8.1%
SPY -30%	-30%	-8%
SPY -50%	-50%	-7.5%

The outcomes are straightforward, the further the market drops, the greater your hedge cushion the losses. If the market rises, your hedge becomes worthless, but your portfolio grows.

The scenarios where you lose are when the market does nothing, but as always you treat the hedge cost as an insurance premium - money well spent for peace of mind.

So if you're concerned that a 1929/2008 style crash could decimate your portfolio, then implementing a hedged position will do wonders for your peace of mind.

> Note: If 3.5% of your portfolio seems too much for a hedge, you can "finance" some of your hedge positions by selling short dated calls on the index. For a more in-depth tutorial of how to do this, you can find it in the bonus resources section at freemanpublications.com/bonus

Managing the Hedge

If the market drops, hedge gains can be sold or rolled. You can use this capital to either fund new stock purchases at depressed prices, or rebalance your hedge. If the market rallies or stays flat, treat the hedge cost as insurance premium - money spent for protection you didn't need but were glad to have.

When to roll is critical, like your long LEAPS calls, roll 60-90 days before expiry, don't let theta eat into your protection. Always extend another 12-18 months to maintain consistent portfolio insurance.

Mistakes to Avoid

Over-hedging by spending 5%+ annually drags performance significantly. Stick to the <4% guideline to balance protection with returns. Avoid buying puts too far OTM - these "cheap lottery" puts rarely pay off when you need them most, because you need the stock to drop enough to cover the cost of your hedge. If you're buying 20% OTM puts, you need the SPY to drop by 21% just to cover the cost of said puts.

Don't use single-stock puts for portfolio hedging. They're expensive, driven by individual company volatility rather than market risk, and too narrow to provide meaningful protection.

Remember this key principle: hedges are not meant to beat the market or provide outperformance. They simply soften the blow. You're not trying to be Michael Burry and make 400% when the market is down 40%, you're just trying to make a 30% drawdown become a 10% drawdown.

Who Shouldn't Hedge

Investors under 30 with long time horizons should focus on saving and compounding rather than hedging. Downturns become buying opportunities when you have decades until retirement. Small portfolios under $100,000 face hedge costs that take too big a bite from returns. It's better to direct cash toward growth at this stage.

The key principle is that hedging is for pre-retirees and retirees who can't afford large drawdowns that would derail their retirement timeline or force them back into the workforce.

Key Takeaways

Hedging equals insurance, not speculation. The best vehicle for most investors is index ETF LEAPS puts on SPY, QQQ, or IWM. Allocate 3-4% annually and roll 60-90 days before expiration to maintain protection.

Don't over-hedge, and don't hedge if you're young or have a small account. The goal is cushioning the blow and preserving discipline during market stress - not timing the market or generating profits from fear.

When implemented correctly, LEAPS put hedges provide the peace of mind that allows you to stay invested during the inevitable market downturns that destroy unprepared investors. They're not exciting, but they work when you need them most.

In the next chapter, we'll explore how to put all these concepts together into a complete LEAPS portfolio management system that can generate consistent returns while managing risk across multiple positions and strategies.

Chapter 10

PSYCHOLOGY & CONVICTION - MASTERING THE MENTAL GAME

It may surprise you (or not) to know that news headlines are getting more negative, even as living standards, lifespans, and technological innovation continue to improve. A 2022 study at UPenn showed that news headlines have steadily gotten more negative over the past 150 years, with a marked acceleration since 2015. A further study by The Brookings Institute showed that this has spilled into people's thoughts about the overall economy and society at large.

This negativity bias then further spills into investing. Even when markets are making new highs, it always *feels* like a crash is looming. The result is that investors live in constant anxiety - selling too early, hesitating to enter good positions, or panic-exiting perfectly sound trades at the worst possible moments.

The punchline is this - conviction isn't about ignoring risk, instead it's about building enough structure into your process that you can tune out the noise and focus on the signals that actually matter for long-term success.

The mechanics of LEAPS are straightforward, but psychology determines your overall outcomes. Markets can shake you out of positions before rewarding you for holding them. Meaning that your real edge comes from consistency and discipline, not from being cleverer than everyone else.

This is especially true with LEAPS, where your holding period spans 12-24 months. You'll experience multiple news cycles, earnings reports, analyst upgrades and downgrades, and general market volatility. Without the right psychological framework, you'll find yourself making emotional decisions that undermine even the best fundamental analysis.

The 4 Pillars of Conviction

True conviction doesn't equal stubbornness. Real conviction comes from having systematic foundations that you can rely on when emotions try to take over, combined with a time horizon that actually works in your favor. In fact, everything you've learned about LEAPS can be broken down into 4 pillars of conviction. If you have all 4 of these, then you'll be in a high conviction state for every trade.

Fundamentals provide your first pillar - you need stock candidates with solid business metrics, not companies riding hype cycles.

Valuation gives you your second pillar - PEG ratios of 1.5 or below and fair entry prices relative to growth rates.

Risk controls form your third pillar - never risking more than 5% of your portfolio on any single position.

Your exit plan becomes the fourth pillar - written in advance with specific criteria, not improvised during stressful moments.

What makes LEAPS uniquely powerful is how they transform patience from a luxury into your primary adjustment tool. Short-term options demand daily decisions because theta decay is relentless - every day that passes without movement costs you money, creating psychological pressure that leads to poor decisions and overtrading. LEAPS lose very little time value in their first 6-12 months, which means when a position moves against you temporarily, your first response can be to simply wait rather than panic into action.

With these four pillars in place and a framework built for months and quarters rather than days and weeks, daily price movements become irrelevant noise rather than emotional triggers. You have an objective system that tells you whether to hold, adjust, or exit based on criteria rather than feelings, aligned with how businesses actually develop and how markets reward long-term thinking.

Signals vs. Noise in Investing

Learning to distinguish between signals and noise is perhaps the most important psychological skill for all investors, but it becomes absolutely critical when you're holding positions for 12-24 months.

Noise includes daily price movements that mean nothing over 18-month time horizons. A 1% drop on Tuesday followed by a 2% rally on Wednesday tells you nothing about whether your medium term investment thesis is correct.

Clickbait financial headlines designed to generate clicks rather than inform decisions flood your news feed with phrases like "Housing market abnormalities are growing" or "Non-essential consumer expenditures are falling."

Analyst upgrades and downgrades that simply reflect recent price movements rather than fundamental changes - notice how upgrades tend to come after stocks have already rallied 20%, and downgrades arrive after they've fallen.

Social media doom-posts and fear-mongering prey on your emotional vulnerabilities with constant predictions of recession, market crashes, or sector collapses. Twitter threads about "the coming collapse of tech stocks" or Reddit posts claiming "this is just like 2008" appear weekly, regardless of actual economic conditions. Even seemingly sophisticated commentary from financial TV often focuses on what happened yesterday rather than what might happen over the next year.

Signals include earnings trends showing consistent revenue, EPS, and free cash flow improvement over multiple quarters. Not just one good or bad quarter, but sustained improvement that suggests business momentum. Valuation metrics relative to peers, historical averages, and growth rates that show whether you're paying a reasonable price for the growth you're expecting. Long-term technical levels like 200-day moving averages and multi-year support and resistance zones that indicate institutional buying or selling patterns.

Business fundamentals provide the strongest signals. Customer growth metrics that reveal whether the business is expanding its reach, competitive moat strength that determines whether advantages are sustainable or temporary. Industry trends that create tailwinds or headwinds lasting years, not months.

Think of it like being a pilot in turbulence. You ignore the shaking and bumping because that's just atmospheric noise that doesn't affect your destination or flight plan. But you react instantly if the engine warning light comes on, because that's a signal indicating something fundamental has changed about your aircraft's ability to complete the journey safely.

The key is training yourself to recognize the difference automatically, so you don't waste emotional energy reacting to every piece of market turbulence while missing the genuine signals that should influence your long-term positions.

Avoiding Hope & Stubbornness

Hope is not a strategy, and stubbornness is not conviction. Real conviction comes from following rules rather than feelings, no matter how uncomfortable that might be in the moment.

If your stop-loss level is hit, you exit the position. You don't lower the stop-loss or rationalize why "this time is different."

If the fundamental thesis breaks down, for example if revenue growth stalls, margins compress, or competitive dynamics shift then you exit <u>regardless of your emotional attachment to the position.</u>

Conversely, if a trade is working in your favor, you follow your predetermined plan for taking profits or rolling positions to lock in gains and extend time. You don't get greedy and abandon your system because you think you can squeeze out a few more percentage points.

Perhaps most importantly, don't take market movements personally or let losses trigger revenge trading. The market doesn't know you exist, doesn't care about your financial goals, and isn't "out to get you" when positions move against you.

When you start thinking "the market owes me" or "I need to make back what I lost," you've shifted from systematic investing to emotional gambling. Revenge trading, like doubling down on losing positions or taking bigger risks to recover losses quickly, destroys more accounts than any other psychological mistake. Each trade should be evaluated independently based on its own merits, not as a way to recover from previous disappointments.

Case Study: Meta at $99

In October 2022, I made my boldest recommendations ever. Meta was trading at $99 per share after falling from highs near $380. The fundamentals were intact - the company still dominated social media with 3 billion daily users, had massive cash flows, and had undermonetized assets like WhatsApp. However, the valuation had become absurdly cheap by any historical measure, and sentiment was overly pessimistic due to concerns about metaverse spending and Apple's privacy changes.

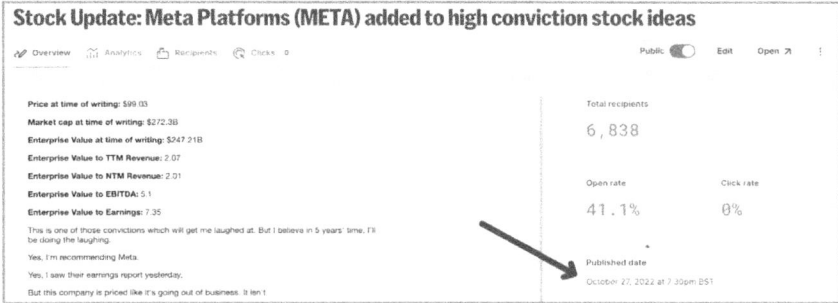

Figure 11: Meta recommendation (Source: Kit.com)

Over the following months, I received numerous messages from readers who had followed the analysis:

"Thanks! I sold at $125 for a big win!"

"I got out at $150 - great call!"

Then, as the stock continued climbing, the tone of the messages completely flipped:

"I can't believe I sold at $125."

"I thought it couldn't go higher."

"I didn't want to lose my profits."

You'll notice that none of these reasons had anything to do with Meta's actual business performance or competitive position. They were emotional, self-centered justifications based on noise rather than signals. The business was continuing to perform well - revenue growth was reaccelerating, margins were expanding, and my WhatsApp monetization prediction was coming true.

Today, Meta trades around $750 per share. The people who sold early based on emotions missed out on massive additional gains, while those who stayed anchored to the fundamental framework captured the full move.

The lesson is clear: in the long run, fundamentals win. Conviction means ignoring the noise and staying anchored to your systematic framework, even when it feels uncomfortable in the short term.

Key Takeaways

Psychology accounts for roughly 80% of your success in LEAPS trading, while strategy and tactics make up the remaining 20%. Conviction doesn't mean hope or stubbornness - it means having a structured, disciplined approach that you can rely on when emotions try to take over.

Patience becomes your first and most powerful adjustment tool with LEAPS. You have time to be right about the big picture even if you're wrong about short-term timing. Learn to distinguish between signals that matter for 18-month outcomes and noise that only creates emotional turbulence.

Your edge comes from staying consistent and disciplined when others are panicking or selling too early based on emotions. The market rewards those who can think in years while others are reacting to daily headlines.

In the final chapter, we'll put everything together into a complete system for building and managing a LEAPS portfolio that can generate consistent returns while keeping you psychologically comfortable with the inevitable ups and downs of long-term investing.

CONCLUSION: YOUR LEAPS JOURNEY STARTS NOW

When I first discovered LEAPS, I thought I'd found a clever way to make more money with less capital. What I actually discovered was something far more valuable: a systematic approach to building wealth that doesn't require me to outsmart the market or time every move perfectly.

The SOXL trade I described in the introduction wasn't the result of superior market timing or insider knowledge. It was the product of having the right framework when opportunity presented itself. Fundamental analysis that identified an overreaction, valuation work that confirmed the opportunity, and LEAPS that gave me the time and leverage to capitalize on it.

That's what this entire book has been about, giving you a complete system for identifying great businesses, buying them at reasonable prices, and using LEAPS to amplify your returns while controlling your risk.

The Power of Systematic Thinking

Every successful LEAPS investor I know follows some version of the framework we've covered.

They start with fundamental analysis to identify companies worth owning for 12-24 months, using the criteria we outlined in chapter 4 and 10-factor scorecard to separate quality businesses from hype-driven stories.

They apply valuation discipline through PEG ratios and historical comparisons, ensuring they're not paying premium prices for average growth.

They structure trades systematically using OptionStrat modeling, targeting 0.80-0.90 delta strikes with 18-24 month expirations while never risking more than 5% per position.

They manage positions through predetermined adjustment rules rather than emotional reactions, rolling when appropriate and exiting when their thesis breaks down.

They enhance returns through strategies like SMCCs when suitable, and protect portfolios through hedging when appropriate.

Above all else, they maintain the psychological discipline to distinguish between signals and noise, staying anchored to their framework when markets try to shake them out of good positions.

What You Can Realistically Expect

LEAPS won't make you rich overnight, and they won't eliminate the normal volatility that comes with equity investing. What they will give you is a systematic way to potentially earn 20-40% annual returns through a combination of capital appreciation and income generation.

More importantly, they'll give you a framework that scales with your account size and doesn't require you to become a full-time trader. Whether you have $25,000 or $500,000 to invest, the principles remain the same. Identify quality businesses, buy them at reasonable prices while using LEAPS for capital efficiency, and have the patience to let your thesis play out.

The income strategies we've covered with SMCCs, can add to your returns while you wait for your long-term positions to mature. While the hedging techniques can help you sleep better during inevitable market downturns.

The Compound Effect

The real power of LEAPS becomes apparent over multiple years. Consider a $100,000 portfolio earning 20% annually through systematic LEAPS investing. After five years, that becomes $248,000. After ten years, it's over $619,000. The combination of capital efficiency, income generation, and compound growth creates wealth-building potential that's difficult to achieve through traditional stock investing alone.

But remember - these returns come from following a systematic process, not from gambling on weekly options or chasing the latest meme stocks. They come from the repetitive work of fundamental analysis, valuation discipline, and risk management that most retail investors skip entirely.

LEAPS work because they align with how great businesses actually create value - over years, not days. They give you the time to be right about the big picture while being wrong about short-term timing. They provide the leverage to amplify returns while defining your risk upfront.

Plus they offer a sustainable approach to wealth building that doesn't require you to predict the unpredictable or time the untimeable. You're not trying to outsmart the market, instead you're trying to participate in the long-term growth of great businesses using the most efficient tools available.

The semiconductor trade that opened this book worked because I had a systematic framework in place when opportunity presented itself. The Meta position at $99 worked for the same reason. Your future successes will come from having that same systematic approach ready when your opportunities arise.

Final Thoughts

The financial media will continue promoting day trading systems and weekly options strategies because they generate more commissions and advertising revenue. Social media will keep pushing get-rich-quick schemes because they attract more followers than systematic wealth building.

But the real money—the life-changing, retirement-securing, generational wealth—comes from boring, systematic approaches like the one we've covered in this book. It comes from identifying great businesses, buying them at reasonable prices, and having the patience to let compound growth work in your favor.

LEAPS give you the tools to do this more efficiently than traditional stock investing. The framework gives you the discipline to do it consistently. The psychology chapter gives you the mental tools to stick with it when markets test your resolve.

Everything you need is in these pages. The only question now is whether you'll have the discipline to implement it systematically rather than looking for shortcuts that don't exist.

Your LEAPS journey starts with your next trade. Make it count.

I hope this book has given you both the knowledge and the confidence to use LEAPS as a powerful wealth-building tool. If there's anything you'd like more clarity on, or if you'd like personalized help applying these strategies inside your portfolio, my team and I are here to support you.

You can reach me anytime at admin@freemanpublications.com or explore more resources at freemanpublications.com/bonus.

And if you found this book valuable, I'd be grateful if you left a review on Amazon. Your feedback helps us improve future projects and reach more investors like you.

To your financial freedom and future success,

Oliver El-Gorr

Founder & CEO, Freeman Publications

ACKNOWLEDGEMENTS

As always, these books are a group effort, and while I get the bulk of the public credit - there are many people behind the scenes worthy of recognition too.

First of all, thanks to Anthony-James Owen whose talk on LEAPS at our inaugural Investormania event in London sparked the demand for this book amongst our own community and for helping me become a better investor through our discussions.

Thanks to Miles Thormodson for his hard work coaching students in our programs, and making sure no stone was left unturned with their questions. Thanks to Shakil Chandran for ensuring I didn't break anything while putting this book together and for knowing where all the images I lost were.

Thanks to Soorej Gopi, Yadukrishnan Adikal and the entire team at Backed-By for their assistance in the formatting, cover design and final checks on the book.

Thank you to all the beta readers whose keen eye and thoughtful feedback made the final of this book the best it could be - a special thanks to Richard Emslie, Ray Morales, Roger Sels, Simon Patmore and Brian Kurcis for their detailed notes

And last but by no means least, thank you to my wife Jemma for always supporting me on projects like this, which at times, can be a labour of love. Also to Jasper and Ivy for bringing more joy to my life than I could ever imagine

Oliver

REFERENCES

Fidelity, (n.d.) – *Leaps and Bounds (Fidelity Viewpoints).* Retrieved from https://www.fidelity.com/viewpoints/active-investor/leaps-and-bounds

FINRA, (n.d.) – *Non-Traditional ETFs FAQ.* Retrieved from https://www.finra.org/rules-guidance/key-topics/etf/non-traditional-etf-faq

Harris, B. & Sojourner, A., 2024 – *Why are Americans so displeased with the economy? (Brookings, January 5, 2024).* Retrieved from https://www.brookings.edu/articles/why-are-americans-so-displeased-with-the-economy/

Novel Investor, (n.d.) – *Annual S&P Sector Returns.* Retrieved from https://novelinvestor.com/sector-performance/

Spencer, J. 2018 – *Triumph of the Market Pessimists* (September 21, 2018). Retrieved from https://www.wsj.com/articles/triumph-of-the-market-pessimists-1537522201

Total Real Returns, 2025 – *XLU: Total Return Chart (with Dividends Reinvested).* Retrieved from https://totalrealreturns.com/n/XLU

van Binsbergen, J. H., Bryzgalova, S., Mukhopadhyay, M., & Sharma, V., 2023 – *(Almost) 200 Years of News-Based Economic Sentiment (SSRN, last revised Dec 19, 2023).* Retrieved from https://papers.ssrn.com/sol3/papers.cfm?abstract_id=4261249

Wellington Management, 2024 - *The importance of capital efficiency in a higher-for-longer rate environment.* Wellington Management, 2024. Available at: https://www.wellington.com/en-us/institutional/insights/importance-of-capital-efficiency-in-higher-for-longer-rate-environment

www.ingramcontent.com/pod-product-compliance
Lightning Source LLC
Chambersburg PA
CBHW030532210326
41597CB00014B/1118

Wen, Y. & Arbogast, I., 2021 – *How COVID-19 Has Impacted Stock Performance by Industry (St. Louis Fed On the Economy, March 21, 2021).* Retrieved from https://www.stlouisfed.org/on-the-economy/2021/march/covid19-impacted-stock-performance-industry